Dyslexia's Competitive Edge

Business and Leadership Insights and Strategies for Dyslexic Entrepreneurs, Business Owners, and Professionals

Tiffay Sunday

TIFFANY SUNDAY

ISBN: 1511542594
ISBN 13: 9781511542593
Library of Congress Control Number: 2015905352
CreateSpace Independent Publishing Platform
North Charleston, South Carolina

Determination

This book is dedicated to all dyslexic individuals past, present, and future.

When I was a child, being dyslexic was hard, and many times I wanted to toss in the towel and call it quits. Yet, I did not.

Teachers, educators, friends, and strangers were always telling me I would not accomplish much in life. Instead, I chose to prove them wrong.

My determination and resiliency developed into unbreakable drive.

Time has taught me that dyslexia is a powerful teacher if we are willing to learn.

My desire to prove people wrong has faded. I now channel my energy into my passions.

We are the visionaries, inventors, and artists. We think differently, see the world differently, and solve problems differently.

It is from these differences that the dyslexic brain derives its brilliance.

Thank You

This book would not have been possible without the following people:

- Skip Howard, you are the coolest entrepreneur I know! Thank You! Your support is invaluable.
- Seth Goldman, co-Founder of Honest Tea, thank you for your time and insight.
- Greg Bustin, my former boss, who is a Vistage speaker and leader. Thank you for reaching out to your network to find professional coaches who are dyslexic or work with dyslexics.
- Heather Hardeman, co-founder of the Dyslexia Parent Network, thank you for your time and for reaching out to the Austin dyslexia community. You were instrumental in making this book possible!
- Gary Smith, founder and CEO of Brainbook Ltd. and creator of the Dyslexia Toolbox, thank you for your support!

- Pat Ryan and daughter Aimee Gordon, thank you for your inspiring story.
- Jeff Govoni and Doug Moran, thank you both for your time and amazing insight on how dyslexia impacts our self-confidence.
- Lauren Ward, thank you for time and support.
- Eric and Heather McGehearty, thank you for your support.
- Ryan Kinzy, thank you! I'll never forget how your one comment validated the book and my mission.
- Ellen O'Neill, Executive Director for the Atlantic Seaboard Dyslexia Education Center, thank you for your support and encouragement.

Contents

Introduction

"Dyslexics are extraordinarily creative about maneuvering their way around problems."
Dr. Julie Logan, Professor at the Cass Business School in London, England

This book provides strategies and advice on how to use your dyslexic brain as a competitive edge in our rapidly changing world. We are experiencing a Digital Renaissance, and many of the talents dyslexics possess are in demand. This book includes insight from my personal experiences and from fellow dyslexic entrepreneurs, business owners, and professionals.

My goal was to create a business strategy and leadership book showcasing the value of dyslexia and how you can maximize your dyslexic brain. I also wrote the book for my son, Brandon, who is dyslexic and a young business owner.

This is the type of book that I wish I had when I was his age: a book which offered strategic guidance on how to use my unique brain. While researching information for the book, I networked my way around the United States and Europe.

Dyslexics are creative, entrepreneurial, and innovative. I believe it is important to **celebrate** our creative talents and focus on our **strengths**. Plenty has been written about the key characteristics of dyslexia. My goal is to share success strategies and leadership insight to help fellow dyslexic business owners and professionals. I believe it is important to share this knowledge and encourage dyslexic individuals.

In high school and college I was discouraged from pursuing my dream of being a journalist, entrepreneur, or screen play writer because of my dyslexia. My parents purchased a personal computer when I was in high school, and for the first time I could independently correct spelling mistakes. The personal computer offered me independence as I wrote, edited, and completed my class assignments.

Even with the new technologies, such as the personal computer and Franklin Speller, I was instructed by my high school counselor to find an easy profession. I was not interested in a boring career. I felt in my gut that the new personal computer would provide dyslexics with a more level playing field and open the door to new opportunities. Experiencing how technology was changing my life, I wanted to do something different.

When I was a teenager, I started businesses, made products to sell, or found other ways to make money. If I was not earning money, I was writing stories, poems, screenplays, or business plans. From these experiences, I developed valuable entrepreneurial skills. When I was a junior in high school, I realized my dyslexic brain had value and was not always a weakness.

Richard Branson, a dyslexic entrepreneur, discussed in his book *Like A Virgin: Secrets They Don't Teach You at Business School* why entrepreneurs and business owners are an important part of our world, from solving complex problems, to hiring employees, to providing a benefit to society. I believe dyslexics can help fuel our economy by starting businesses and finding hidden opportunities.

As technology rapidly advances, the demand for creative, visionary, outside-the-box thinkers will continue to increase. In our highly competitive business environment, dyslexia can provide an advantage. Our dyslexic brains enable us to identify patterns and think in the abstract. **Most importantly, dyslexia enables us to solve complex problems.**

This book provides strategies and insights on how dyslexic entrepreneurs, business owners, and professionals can capitalize on the value of dyslexia.

Why Dyslexics Make Great Entrepreneurs

*"Dyslexics think differently. They are
intuitive and excel at problem solving, seeing
the big picture, and simplifying. They are
poor rote reciters but inspired visionaries."*
Dr. Sally Shaywitz, *Overcoming Dyslexia*

Dyslexics do not fit into a box, circle, or specific definition. One thing is usually true: we are unique, creative thinkers who see the world differently and process information in squiggly pathways in nanoseconds.

Researchers, educators, and scientists study the reason why a large percentage of dyslexics are drawn to business ownership. Dr. Julie Logan, a professor of entrepreneurship at the Cass Business School in London, England, surveyed business owners in the United States to determine how many were dyslexic or identified themselves as having dyslexia. Logan found 35 percent of United States business owners surveyed were dyslexic.

She also noted in her study dyslexics were twice as likely to delegate authority, and excel in verbal communication and problem solving.

In a presentation Logan gave in London, she mentioned the ability to build amazing teams provides dyslexic entrepreneurs and business owners with a significant competitive advantage. She found that the dyslexics she interviewed and surveyed had a higher level of emotional intelligence which allowed them to be empathic with their team members.

Logan also mentioned dyslexics develop strategies early in life to mitigate their weaknesses; these strategies include learning to identify trustworthy people and delegating major responsibilities.

Most educational experts and researchers believe 10 percent of the American population is dyslexic. The statistics are similar in the United Kingdom. I have recently connected with dyslexic entrepreneurs and business owners in England and Scotland and have included information for European readers.

Think about the numbers for a moment. Researchers estimate that 35 percent of dyslexic individuals are business owners, and 10 percent of the total population has dyslexia. When the math is calculated, we have a very large community of dyslexic business owners!

I visited with Seth Goldman, co-founder of Honest Tea, earlier this year. Seth, along with his partner Barry Nalebuff, launched the company in 1998. Honest Tea was later sold to Coca-Cola. Goldman wrote a blog post about the relationship between dyslexia and entrepreneurship. He stated, "I gained a new insight into the value of dyslexia for entrepreneurs." This insight was gained while visiting with entrepreneurs in Madison, Wisconsin during a startup event. He has family members who are dyslexic. Seth noticed the reason why these enterprises were started was because of the creative insight from the dyslexic founders. The founders viewed the world differently. From this difference Seth gained an insight on how dyslexia can benefit entrepreneurs. He said his book, *Mission in a Bottle*, was popular with dyslexic founders.

When I was 12 and running a successful babysitting business, it never occurred to me the skills I was learning would benefit me later. I was curious, bored, and seeking a way to make money. Having an income and a successful small business helped my self-confidence and gave me an outlet outside of school. I did not realize all the difficulties I experienced in school, from the teachers who did not believe in dyslexia, to the students making fun of my spelling, or lack of social skills, would be invaluable training for business ownership.

When I was in grade school, I knew of one or two famous dyslexics. However, in those days there were few, if any, articles about the relationship between dyslexia and entrepreneurship.

Seth Goldman also noted three prized traits of every entrepreneur most of us acquired during school as dyslexic students.

- **Dealing with adversity and bouncing back from daily setbacks.**
- **Seeing existing structures from a completely new perspective.**
- **Being creative and persistent at finding solutions.**

Yep, that's us! This is still an everyday occurrence for most dyslexics. Richard Branson, a dyslexic entrepreneur, often speaks about dyslexia and how it played a pivotal role in launching his first business.

Innovation is the act or process of inventing or introducing something new. From my personal experience and stories shared by fellow dyslexic business owners, our brains are all about innovation. We are constantly seeking a better way to process our environment or create strategies to help us manage our daily demands.

I am not surprised by the multiple studies, business assessments, and educational surveys which continue to demonstrate the connection between dyslexia and entrepreneurship. For many of the dyslexic CEOs and business founders I visited with for the book, this assessment is a no-brainer.

Based on the statistics, teaching entrepreneurship to dyslexic students is crucial.

Thomas G. West addressed teaching entrepreneurship to dyslexics in his book *In the Mind's Eye*.

"However, it should be emphasized that it is no small significance to find – within a study targeting traits among highly successful individuals in business – that the most common trait is, in fact, dyslexia. Consequently, in view of the study results, it would appear that teachers, researchers, and educational planners should find ways to balance their efforts in reading and spelling and help their dyslexic students to develop, as early as possible, high-level business and entrepreneurial skills."

The brilliance within the dyslexic brain is finally being recognized by the business world and public education system. As our world continues to rapidly change, the growing demand for dyslexics and our highly creative, out-of-the-box thinking skills will increase at an exponential rate.

Understanding the value of dyslexia and how our skills will be a critical part of the future is quickly becoming a necessity.

From Failure, the Layers of Resiliency are Added

*"Those who have a 'why' to live,
can bear with almost any 'how'."*
Viktor E. Frankl, *Man's Search for Meaning*

Dyslexia has taught me to never give up. Regardless of the obstacles, I always keep moving forward. At an early age, I knew deep down if I tossed in the towel I knew I would be selling myself short.

For most of us, our resiliency training starts in kindergarten and with each school year, another layer of resiliency is added. I failed frequently in school and was constantly bouncing back from defeats, failures, and mistakes. Over time, I developed immunity to failure. By the time I reached college, the fear of failure had been eliminated. I perfected my problem solving skills as I was always thinking of new ways to mitigate my weaknesses associated with dyslexia.

When I was in grade school, many of my teachers did not understand dyslexia or believe dyslexia was real. Each day I was sent to the resource room to learn knitting while the boys learned phonetics. The special education teachers in grade school did not give my parents much hope and thought finding a husband would be the best approach.

Yet, little did they know, a seed to succeed had been planted and was growing. Each year, as I worked through the obstacles, I discovered my strengths.

Fourth grade was my hardest year. My teacher believed dyslexia was an excuse for not working hard in school. Each day she would ridicule or embarrass me in front of the class. She often mentioned how far behind I was in reading or spelling as compared to my peers. Then one day I mentally drew a line in the sand and decided to prove her wrong. I studied and worked hard on my math assignments. My goal was to be one of the top students in the class. I refused to let her break my spirit or convince me I was dumb.

Each night, I practiced my multiplication tables until I could complete her math quizzes in minutes. By spring, I was the fastest student in class and the best student in math for the remainder of the year. This accomplishment boosted my confidence. In fourth grade, I added multiple layers of resiliency. Most important of all, I learned to have faith in myself, and that with hope, anything was possible.

I believe dyslexics, starting in grade school, develop an amazing reserve of tenacity which can be tapped when needed. This is one of the reasons why I think dyslexics can succeed against the odds. For example, Barbara Corcoran is a dyslexic business owner and a Shark Tank investor. She mentioned during an interview how she actually felt more comfortable when faced with a challenge. There are times, even now, when dyslexia can be very frustrating, especially when I cannot determine how to spell a specific word.

While writing this book, I spent days searching for the correct spelling for the word succinct. None of my technology tools came close to finding the correct spelling, but I was determined to use the word and finally found it. Succinct was added to my note cards of other frequently misspelled words.

I have typed the words entrepreneur and entrepreneurship many times, yet my brain still cannot spell these words correctly. Even with all the frustrations I have experienced, I would never change my dyslexic brain. The creative energy and ability to visually solve problems has always outweighed the frustrations.

Our tough skin and gritty character traits give us the strength we need to push through challenges. For many of us, entrepreneurship, business ownership, or self employment feels more natural than corporate employment. Being your own boss may offer more opportunities to use your dyslexic brain as a competitive edge than a corporate position. As business owners, we can select teams, delegate tasks, and pursue creative ventures.

I tell my son when he is faced with a dyslexia road bump the experience will benefit him in his business and later in life. I have watched him talk with potential customers for hours pitching and selling his products. He is learning that selling to strangers can be hard, especially when you continually hear *"no thank you."* It is not easy, but Brandon knows the experience he is gaining is invaluable. We are a resilient group of individuals, and we understand what it takes to make things happen. Our ability to keep going and to push through failure is an advantage, regardless of our profession. My resiliency was tested again when I was a student at Texas A&M University. One of my professors did not believe dyslexia existed and thought it was a crutch.

The fourth week of the semester, he read my 504 letter to the class which listed my accommodations. When he finished reading the letter, he called me dumb and kicked me out of the class. The university disciplined the professor for his actions.

While discussing my complaint with the Liberal Arts Dean, I requested an exemption from my foreign language requirement. This request was granted, and I completed the required hours with additional classes related to my political science minor.

After the dust settled, I realized I must become an advocate for myself and fellow dyslexic students. I became more open about being dyslexic since I had been previously taught to hide the "disability."

Once again, I added more layers of resiliency and gained confidence in my ability to stand on my own two feet. Overall, the Texas A&M Disabilities Services Department did a great job, and the director and his staff were always supportive. I learned you cannot always fear what others think or believe, especially when you tell them you are dyslexic. I love Seth Godin's quote in his manifesto *Stop Stealing Dreams,* "Passion can overcome fear – the fear of losing, of failing, of being ridiculed." Without passion, it can be difficult to muster the strength to move past our fears and failures.

A side note on fear – fear of any kind leaves you immobile, and nothing happens when fear keeps you from moving forward. Most of our fears are tied to our intelligence or feeling less worthy than our non-dyslexic peers. My fear of not being smart enough has impeded my business pursuits more than my fear of failure.

Richard Branson wrote in his book *Like a Virgin* the "ability to bounce back after a setback is probably the single most important trait an entrepreneurial venture can possess."

The ability to bounce back is critical.

My first job out of college was selling office equipment in the Houston Ship Channel area. Our sales manager told us sales was a numbers game, and selling required a certain number of "no's" to get to a "yes" to produce a sale. The resiliency and tough skin I developed in school gave me the strength to cold call 500 businesses and receive a "no" each time.

Once I understood selling products was a numbers game, I viewed each cold call as an opportunity to meet someone new. By changing my perception of the selling process, I was able to use my strengths to become a top-ranked sales person.

Do not fear failure! Remember each failure or challenge adds another layer of resiliency. Our strong fortitude is a significant competitive edge as we have the strength and patience to find solutions and launch new businesses under duress.

The Power of the Dyslexic Pivot

"With an almost mythological vision – a hope of what could be, with a goal that few others can see."
Steven Blank, *The Four Steps to The Epiphany*

Pivot is a frequently used word in the tech startup industry. In a nutshell, you pivot when you systemically test theories and make changes based on the feedback.

For entrepreneurs and startups, pivoting can be a painful process as the team seeks to find the right market niche, customer, or business model. From our days in elementary school, dyslexics have become skilled at pivoting both in our careers and personal lives. We are constantly testing different tools, components, and strategies to find the best way to use our dyslexic brain.

For example, I know my pain points: spelling, small talk, and inverting information. As a dyslexic business owner, single parent, and mother of a dyslexic teen, I am always pivoting. I test theories or processes subconsciously because pivoting has become an intrinsic part of my dyslexic brain.

I believe our strong pivoting abilities strengthen our problem solving skills because we quickly interchange elements to find which solution works best. In many ways, the dyslexic brain operates similar in function to a tech startup. I believe our ability to pivot is a contributing factor to why 35% of dyslexics are business owners.

A startup tests an idea in the market, and if customers do not like the idea, the founders will pivot until the market niche is found. This is rarely an easy process. I can appreciate Steven Blank's explanation of why it is hard for startups to prove their product or business model. His description could easily be interchanged with how dyslexics think and find a solution.

Blank says, "Founding entrepreneurs are out to prove their vision and business are real and not some hallucination; to succeed, they must abandon the status quo and strike out on what appears to be a new path, often shrouded in uncertainty. Obstacles, hardships, and disasters lie ahead, and their journey to success tests more than financial resources. It tests their stamina, agility, and the limits of courage."

Dyslexic business owners and entrepreneurs can use their dyslexic brain to pivot their business model or services to find hidden opportunities and new markets. Since school, we have quickly learned how to identify patterns of success and eliminate patterns of failure.

Encountering challenges, roadblocks, and closed doors is generally an everyday norm for us, and with each new challenge, we add a layer of resiliency. Just as startups constantly work to validate their product, target market, or business model, dyslexics work constantly to pivot and find solutions for complex problems at work and to manage their personal demands.

Pivot or Persevere

In his book *The Lean Startup* Eric Ries advised startups to have a pivot or persevere meeting because the decision to pivot can be emotionally charged for startups and their founders. For many business owners and founders, determining when to pivot or stay the course can be a difficult decision. For most dyslexics, we learned in school when to pivot and when to persevere through the mud hole.

We can use our knowledge and experience to determine when to pivot or persevere. Our ability to see the big picture and recognize patterns gives us the opportunity to discover emerging business trends. We can determine if these news trends can benefit our businesses or careers. Utilizing this knowledge to make a decision on when to pivot can provide tremendous value to our businesses.

As a business owner, I use my pivoting skills to adapt my company's services to the changing market place. The company was launched in 2004, and at that time we provided traditional marketing services to small businesses and startups. In 2007, when social media marketing was gaining in popularity, instead of persevering and offering traditional marketing services, we pivoted the company's direction. We shifted from being a marketing services company to a product development and marketing strategy company.

Secondly, I felt the profit margins on social media marketing would not provide the growth we were seeking, and I knew my dyslexic brain and real time communication were not compatible. I could visually see how social media would create a major disruption in the marketing, advertising, and media industries. The decision to pivot proved to be a wise choice as our revenue in 2008 increased by 42%.

Thoughts to Consider:
- Think about the future for a moment.
- Use your imagination to envision the future and what technological advancements could impact your business or career. We are at the tip of the iceberg for technologies such as nanotech, biotech, and 3-D manufacturing.
- What positive or negative trends do you see?
- Do you see new markets emerging and/or opportunities for groundbreaking discoveries?
- Can your business pivot to capitalize on these new markets? Or should your business elect to stay the course?
- Which decision will help your business remain competitive and profitable?

How to Duplicate Success

When dyslexics pivot, we base our decisions on past experiences, knowledge gained, and our gut intuition. When a product, venture, or business model does not work, it is best to review and determine why the failure occurred.

To our benefit, the dyslexic brain operates like a sonar device, constantly seeking a solution and faster way to process information.

I learned early in school that for me to be successful, developing strategies for duplicating success was crucial. If not, I would fall further behind in school. For most of us these strategies have become part of our brain's processing system and go unnoticed. Spend a few minutes thinking about the strategies you used in school to duplicate success.

Determine if there are any strategies you are currently not using that could benefit your business or career.

Experiencing failure frequently in school enabled us to learn from our experiences and use the fail fast strategy to quickly determine what worked and what did not work. Developing strategies to compensate for our weaknesses was a necessity, and for many of us, it is still a necessity today.

When fail fast became a popular startup business mantra several years ago, it was hailed as the new Holy Grail strategy. For many dyslexic entrepreneurs, this strategy may feel more comfortable than other business strategies as fail fast and pivoting are more familiar.

Understanding how to duplicate success in a business is critically important for ensuring long term sustainability.

We have learned since grade school our areas of success and how to duplicate them. Our high tolerance for "failure" is an advantage when used wisely. I am more curious and willing to test new ideas and concepts than most of my professional friends and business associates. Dyslexics generally think, "How can I solve this problem?" or "Can I make this process or product better?" We focus on finding a solution rather than worrying about, "What if I fail?"

Our strong ability to solve problems is another asset on our dyslexia balance sheet. Several dyslexic professionals mentioned they love the challenge of solving complex problems. When you pursue a new venture or idea, taking uncalculated risks which could negatively impact your business or career is unwise.

It behooves us to have a plan or strategy in place to offset the potential downside of the venture. I have learned to recognize when a problem is unsolvable and not worth the time. There comes a point to cut bait and save resources.

Thoughts to Consider:
- Can your strategies for duplicating success be used in all practice areas?
- Will these strategies continue to work in our rapidly changing economy and competitive business environment?

Dyslexics wrote the book on how to pivot.

We can see the big picture, understand the problem solving process, and know which components should be changed and which ones should be left alone. Most of us pivot subconsciously. We do not realize how fast we test different solutions or theories. Our ability to pivot rapidly and determine which method will work best is a huge advantage.

Passion is a Prerequisite

*"If you pursue your passions, your visions will be more
likely to become successful realities."*
Richard Branson

Our passion is the internal flame and guiding light that
enables us to develop our ideas into a business, product,
or career. Kevin Mann, founder and CTO of Graphic.ly,
talks about how passion has to be part of the equation.
"If you're not passionate about what you're doing, it won't
mean enough to you to succeed. Startup founders choose
an insanely difficult path, so passion is a prerequisite."
    For dyslexics, our passions support us during difficult
times when nothing seems to work right. I believe we
have a deeper understanding of our innate passion. **Our
passions provide the motivation needed to propel us
past the many obstacles we encounter.** We have a passion for creating and a drive to achieve what has never
been done before.
    Passion is different than loving what you do. I love
doing many things, but I am only passionate about two

things – creative freedom and entrepreneurship. Passion stays even after the love of doing something fades or becomes old. Our curious dyslexic brain takes us down the road less traveled where we can explore different subjects. Understanding the difference is important. Loving what you do may not always generate a profit or income.

I agree with Mann, passion is a requirement and I believe that you cannot fake passion. We either have passion to pursue something or not. My favorite quote from *Star Wars: The Empire Strikes Back* is when Yoda says, "Do or do not, there is no try."

Dream Big or Go Home!

*"If you are going to dream then dream big,
why spend time dreaming small?"*
A tweet I posted for my son.

Have you ever noticed how big dreams make some people nervous? You are visiting with your neighbors or friends and mention an idea beyond anything ever discussed, and the next thing you know, everyone is telling you it will not work.

Troy Marshall is a rancher and blogger for *Beef Magazine* who wrote the blog post "My Secret to Life is to Dream Big & Think Positive." The post was about the importance of "creating a vision and dream that is larger than yourself." Marshall went on to say "motivation can be influenced by outside sources, but the harsh reality is that it is largely self-determined."

Ever since I was diagnosed with dyslexia, I have been told my dreams were too big; that I should not think about being an author to avoid disappointment. Little did they know, I already knew disappointment well, in fact, we were best friends.

My son has already been told several times that his dream of launching an innovative auto company is too big and that his dream should be smaller. Interestingly, we are not alone as others in the dyslexic community have been told the same thing. I do not understand why people discourage a dyslexic student or another person, for that matter.

Our internal dreams are our motivation. My family would often tell me to focus on things I could accomplish to avoid being disappointed, but in reality, they were advising based on *their* fear of being disappointed, not mine. Dyslexics learn about disappointment early and develop a strong faith in their abilities. We are fully aware that most people underestimate our talents. Included in our self-motivation are thoughts about our big dreams and how we can achieve them.

What type of fear is triggered when a dyslexic person or individual shares a big dream or idea? Instead of explaining all the reasons why you would not be interested, ask how they plan to accomplish the dream. I know from experience and listening to others the real value is in the process or strategy dyslexics use to accomplish their dreams.

Because dyslexics by nature think differently, at times it can be difficult for our peers and family members to understand our thought process.

What do you think about all day? Are your thoughts positive or negative? Do you listen to the naysayers or do you focus on your internal motivation? Ralph Waldo

Emerson explained our dreams and positive thoughts the best when he said, "We are what we think about all day long." When I was a teenager, my friends and I talked about our dreams and goals. Since that time, regardless of where I have been in my career, I continued to dream about becoming an author and having my own business. I never gave up on my dream of becoming an author.

Imagination is the Root of Innovation

We use our dreams and imagination to think of alternative ways to solve highly complex problems. As Albert Einstein wrote, "**Our imagination is more important than knowledge.**" From our imagination, we can see the future and envision the possibilities. The majority of the articles written about dyslexic entrepreneurs and businesses owners mention how we use our dreams and imagination to develop new products and start innovative businesses. Webster's dictionary defines being visionary as "thinking about or planning the future with imagination."

Thinking about the future using our imagination is part of the dyslexia DNA. There are many dyslexics past and present who have used their visionary skills to make discoveries that changed the world.

Steve Jobs was a gifted visionary thinker. His speech at the 2005 Stanford graduation ceremony is one of my favorites. If you have not seen this video on YouTube, I highly recommend viewing the speech. Dyslexic visionaries often ask "Why" and "What if." To use our visionary skills to our benefit, it is important to take time to daydream and imagine the future. With the rapid advancements in technology, it is hard for many people to visualize what the world will look like in 2020 or 2050.

Using our imagination enables us to find solutions for complex problems and customer pain points. During the time when I was editing this book, I went to an estate sale and found a large old book with over 1,000 drawings and notes by Leonardo da Vinci. It reminded me why he was the ultimate visionary. His drawings and detailed notes are amazing. Leonardo studied all the major subjects and was also a gifted artist. He was a true Renaissance Man. Visionary thoughts occur when our brains have time to think, study different subjects, and ponder what is possible just like da Vinci did.

Most dyslexics daydream and think in the abstract more than non-dyslexics. Our ability to imagine the future and to create new products, processes, or inventions is one of the biggest advantages of dyslexia. Skip Howard, a dyslexic entrepreneur and inventor, made an interesting point about how a vision is derived from our imagination. When he has a concept vision, he can see the finished product. He said, "I know how something will work in the end and then back into the problem. I know – I will find a way to make it work."

Skip's imagination is at the root of his inventions. He is currently working on developing interactive writing paper which will be the tipping point for creating smart spaces. His goal is to create interactive physical walls that will have artificial intelligence (AI). Having AI will enable the smart space to understand contextual interactions, such as a person's mood or personal preferences.

The smart space can make necessary adjustments based on previously established settings and environmental input. The person can also interact with the wall and give commands. Skip sees how the smart space technology can be used to improve patient care in hospitals or change the way we shop at the grocery store.

Einstein stated, "We cannot solve our problems with the same level of thinking that created them."

By imaging the future, we can discover solutions to problems that cannot be solved with our current way of thinking. As our world continues to change, the need for dyslexic visionaries and imaginative thinking will increase. Computers and robots will evolve to manage advanced accounting and financial tasks currently performed by mid-level managers and staff members. To stay competitive, companies will continue to seek visionary strategic advice and/or hire employees with visionary talents. Dyslexics can add tremendous value to a business or organization in these practice areas.

Last month, I read J. Peder Zane article, "If You Can Know It All, How Come You Don't?" in *The New York Times*. Zane discussed how mass open online courses and the abundance of information was impacting our knowledge level. The overwhelming amount of information and our focus on specialized careers and research fields may, in fact, cause us to know less. Zane quoted David Galenston, a Professor of Economics from the University of Chicago.

Galenston noted that our "progress often hinges on those rare individuals who escape its (knowledge) bonds. Artists from Picasso to Bob Dylan to entrepreneurs, including Bill Gates and Steve Jobs, changed the world by radically finding new ways of looking at old problems. They cut through all the accumulated stuff – forget what's been done – to see something special, something new."

Most dyslexics are gifted visionaries and dreamers who can cut through the old ways and find a completely new way to solve an old problem.

Finding the downtime for your dyslexic brain to think and explore is important.

If your schedule is full, then combine your visionary thinking and daydreaming time with exercise. Go for a run without your electronic device, or take the dog for a walk: just find time to allow your brain freedom to think, create, and dream.

Daydreaming and creative thinking are the roots of innovation and discovery and **should not be undervalued**. I seriously doubt anyone has told Elon Musk, founder of Tesla, that his dreams are too big! With each and every one of our accomplishments, the world can see firsthand the value of dyslexia.

Trust Your Gut Intuition

"My gut instinct is something I rely on every day."
Jo Malone, Founder of Jo Malone Cosmetics

Every dyslexic person I interviewed mentioned their gut intuition. In some cases, business owners knew the answer to the problem, yet could not tell me how they knew the answer. When my son was young, I would tell him to "trust your gut." He would reply "it's not saying anything" and would become frustrated that he never "heard" his gut.

Now he is older and has learned to listen to his gut intuition. I have developed strategies for managing my dyslexia, and like family traditions, trusting your gut intuition is one of the strategies I have passed along to my son.

Learning to listen to your gut intuition is important. Everyone has a natural instinct; it helps us stay safe when we encounter a dangerous situation. I believe our dyslexic brain processes multisensory environmental cues faster than our non-dyslexic peers, which strengthens our natural instinct. Since grade school, we have used our gut intuition to quickly assess potential team members, answer questions, and make business decisions. There have been times in my life that I have chosen to go against my gut feeling only to regret my decision later.

One time, during a meeting with a new startup client, I had an uneasy feeling. I could feel that something was not right, but could not put my finger on why. As we worked on the engagement agreement, my uneasiness increased.

Several times during one conversation I caught inconsistencies in the founder's story, and when asked, he told me I heard him wrong. Most dyslexics are power listeners as we rely heavily on our listening skills. To make a long story short, my gut was correct. I realized after two months of work with this new client that I had made a mistake. The founder had no intention of paying us for our services. I terminated the agreement immediately, which resulted in a financial loss for the company.

Three months later, I learned that his co-founder was in jail and that he might be involved as well. This experience reminded me again of the importance of listening to my gut intuition. Now when I feel uneasy about a business situation or person, I take the time to determine what is at the root of my uneasiness.

Jo Malone founded Jo Malone Cosmetics, a London-based company, in the 1990s. She talked about how she used her gut intuition in an interview with *The New York Times*. She stated, "My instinct is telling me one thing and reality is telling something else. I rely on my gut instinct all the time in business. If something doesn't feel right, I'm not going to do it, which can be very tricky in a team and in a small business." Making decisions by gut feeling or by seeing something in our minds can be hard for our peers and teammates to understand.

I spoke with Pat Ryan, a retired dyslexic entrepreneur and business owner. Pat was the owner of multiple Budget Rent a Car franchises in Texas. During our conversation, he mentioned how he relied on his gut to make business decisions, hire employees, and to expand the business. Pat often tells people **"if you do not have dyslexia – get it!"** Early in his life he was able to grasp the value of dyslexia and use his talents to build a successful business. I had the opportunity to interview his daughter, Aimee Gordon, who is dyslexic and has a successful career in sales. Like her father, she relies on her intuition to make decisions.

My intuition was put to the test again last year when a startup coordinator called about booking me as a keynote speaker for a new startup organization. The lady was very friendly; however, she kept asking questions about a project of mine and would not provide an event date.

After 15 minutes my gut told me she was fishing for information, and that she had no intention of booking me as the speaker. I politely told her to call when the group had an event date and ended the call. Three week later, I received an email announcing the speaker with an invitation to the event.

Not all gut intuitions are based on negative vibes. I have also experienced a strong gut intuition to call someone I needed to speak with and who was impossible to reach. When I listen to my gut, I am able to connect with the individual. There are also times when I have a hunch to pursue an opportunity. After receiving my MBA, I was interviewing for a marketing strategy position. Bustin & Co. was one of the companies that I was considering. A competitor had offered a better compensation package; however, my gut kept telling me to select Bustin, which proved to be my best employment decision to date. Working with Greg Bustin and my team was an amazing opportunity.

I believe part of our intuition includes what Dr. Cloud calls the Cringe Factor. In his book, *9 Simple Things You Must Do,* Dr. Cloud discusses why the Cringe Factor is important. A client of his stated, "My rule is this: anytime I have to cringe or take a big gulp to agree to do anything substantial with anyone, whether to hire him, work with him, or anything significant, I don't do it. I won't go forward as long as the cringe factor is there. Period."

The Cringe Factor is part of our gut intuition.

For dyslexics, we often rely on gut intuition to make decisions, select team members, and build our businesses or careers. When you feel that something is not right about a new business partner, investor or client, ask yourself what could be causing your uneasy feeling.

Questions to Consider:
- Is it something they said?
- Are you picking up on inconsistencies in their story, or do they feel "too slick?"

- From a market or business perspective: Do you get a gut feeling that changes are occurring in your industry? While others continue to ignore these trends your gut is screaming "Something major has changed!"
- Or, do you get a gut feeling encouraging you to pursue a new opportunity?

The Cringe Factor has value. It is important to recognize your gut feeling and how it can help you save money, time, and frustration.

Conversely, learning to listen and trust your gut when it says "Go" is equally important. I have learned to respect my gut intuition, and when I hear it telling me to pick up the phone, send an email, or pursue a project, **I do it!**

Build a Team of
People You Trust

"Trust Can Scale."
Chris Moody, President and COO of Gnip

For dyslexic business owners and professionals, our number one priority is building a team of people we can trust. Having a solid team of professionals that share our vision and understand dyslexia is crucial. For us, delegating tasks, projects, or major practice areas is essential.

I spoke with Aimee Gordon about building good teams. She is an account director who is responsible for two Fortune 500 client sales teams. Aimee talked about how she developed her strong team building abilities in high school.

Her strategies included surrounding herself with fellow students who could answer her questions and provide copies of class notes. She also mentioned that she learned early to delegate and often took the role as team leader. Aimee discussed the importance of finding good team members who could mitigate her weaknesses, especially the dysgraphia.

All my life I have built formal and informal teams with co-workers and business partners who could help compensate for my weaknesses related to dyslexia. When I worked as a compliance specialist at FINRA, a regulatory agency, my job required that I write formal case reports.

I partnered with two team members whom I could trust to review my reports for any major spelling or grammar mistakes. To return the favor, I offered to help my team members in areas where my dyslexic brain excelled, such as big picture thinking and problem solving.

As you build your business teams and professional networks, choose individuals who will compliment your strengths and moderate your weaknesses. For example, if reading contracts and proposals is tedious for you, find an expert who can summarize the key points. Pat Ryan, a retired entrepreneur and business owner, talked about the importance of professional teams.

He bartered services in exchange for help with reading and understanding the business contracts associated with the initial purchase of his first Budget Rent a Car franchise.

Teams that share the same goals and vision perform better. When searching for new team members, seek individuals who share the same passion and understand dyslexia. Nothing deflates yours or your group's energy faster than explaining or justifying the company's mission and purpose. There are times when we are unable to select individuals that are 100 percent supportive of our dyslexia.

When possible, speak with the team member about the matter or seek guidance from an executive coach or mentor. Role playing can help as well. I have found from personal experience that saying nothing does not help the situation, and now I let new business partners or associates know that I am dyslexic.

Our teams become our corporate and professional families. For any business to grow or scale, trust is a must.

For startups, teams can make or break the business. When building your team, remember your value and what you bring to the table. Think about what type of person deserves your trust. Chris Moody, president and COO of Gnip, wrote a guest post on Brad Feld's blog. Moody wrote, "Startups that experience success are typically built upon a strong foundation of trust among the early founders/employees. One of the biggest mistakes startups make is replacing trust with a process, which can rip the heart right out of your company." Moody closed the post by stating, "Trust could be one of your most valuable company assets. As a leader, you need to fight like hell to protect it."

I know from launching a startup that hiring good team members you can trust is a necessity. When I interview candidates, I do three things: seek individuals who are passionate, individuals who have a positive attitude, and then rely on my gut intuition to make a decision. I've learned that employees and team members can be trained or taught new skills.

However, trust is a different matter as it cannot be taught or learned. An individual either has integrity or they do not. As Director of Marketing for Meals to Live, an investor funded startup, I hired interns that we could trust. The interns proved to be instrumental in the company's growth.

Doug Moran, an executive coach, discussed the importance of building informal teams, especially for self-employed professionals and small business owners. Building a team of professionals who can mitigate your weaknesses can help improve and grow your business. For self-employed professionals, delegating services to contractors or service providers who can handle areas such as editing, accounting, and implementing your strategy can greatly benefit your business.

Building a strong personal network is important. Remember to develop an informal group of friends and supporters who can offer encouragement during tough times. I have two close friends with whom I share my frustrations and disappointments. In return, they offer encouragement and help when needed.

Electing to inform new clients and business partners about your dyslexia is a personal decision. Finding the right time to inform new business partners that I am dyslexic has been most effective. Last year, I added the information to my professional profile. I have experienced a freedom of having the information "out there", as hiding my dyslexia provided no benefit.

Often times, hiding the information was a hindrance as I found myself dancing around the matter, which created more problems. One client asked if I was hiding something. Now they know I am dyslexic. I would like to add that even today there can still be a negative stigma associated with dyslexia, and not all corporations or managers understand.

Being a business owner, I have a different level of freedom in speaking about my dyslexia. Because I have experienced discrimination while being employed at a large corporation, I understand that corporate employees may not have the ability to disclose their dyslexia. I recommend that you speak with a professional coach or an attorney who specializes in 504 disabilities if you plan to disclose this information to your employer.

To strengthen your team building skills, work with an executive coach and attend workshops or conferences to learn new strategies that will enhance your strong skills.

The Importance of a Good Mentor or Executive Coach

"Whenever I am asked what is the missing link between a promising businessperson and a successful one mentoring comes to mind."
Richard Branson, *The Importance of Mentoring* Blog post

Dr. Julie Logan, a dyslexia expert and business professor, discovered from her research that finding a good coach or mentor was crucial for dyslexic startup founders. The greatest benefit was finding a good mentor who could help from the time the company was formed and launched.

Finding a mentor you can trust and who can provide feedback is invaluable. I have worked with three executive coaches during my career and their insight has always been helpful.

For this book I interviewed Doug Moran, who is dyslexic and an executive coach. We talked about how a coach is neutral and can observe behaviors or thought processes that we may not notice. He mentioned that dyslexic professionals can feel broken and have personal baggage from their childhood that affects their self-confidence. A coach who understands dyslexia can provide guidance on how to handle negative habits we may have developed.

Five years ago I had the opportunity to work with a Vistage Chair and Leadership Coach. She offered guidance on how I could increase my confidence and reduce the insecurities I developed in school. My coach said that being aware of these emotions allows us the ability to manage our feelings and behaviors more effectively.

When I felt insecure, she recommended that I think about what I had accomplished as an adult. During our last session, my coach suggested I inform my clients and business partners about my dyslexia. She believed the "negative baggage" was doing more harm than good. When I informed my clients and business partners about my dyslexia, I learned they knew people who were dyslexic.

In addition to feeling insecure, another common dyslexic behavioral habit is telling individuals our accomplishments when we initially meet them, such as during a business introduction. This habit was probably created during our childhood when we had to defend our intelligence. I previously had this habit.

As I matured, the need to prove my intelligence faded. Managing our childhood baggage may require the help of a trained therapist. Being aware of how our childhood experiences can impact our life and career is important.

With the help of my coaches, I have learned to value my time more and know that I am not defective.

Executive Leadership Coach Jeff Govoni has experience working with dyslexic executives and professionals. I talked with Jeff about how coaching can benefit dyslexics. He said that coaching helps dyslexics change their perception of being broken to creating an updated mental image based on their adult life and successes. We also discussed how the drive to prove everyone wrong provided the determination we needed to make it through school.

However, this same determination can backfire as we mature. Three years ago I went after a goal that was based on the "prove them wrong" premise. Several months into my charge up the mountain I realized this thinking no longer motivated me. The "prove them wrong" thought process felt dated and out of place. My gut was telling me to focus on what mattered most instead of proving someone wrong.

I needed the "show them" determination in school and college or I would not have graduated. Now, whenever I feel dumb, I think about my accomplishments. This journey has not been easy. I still feel a sting when someone challenges my intelligence or when the need to "show them" crops up. However, I have learned that while it is part of who I am, it no longer owns me.

Take the time to find a good mentor or coach who understands dyslexia and/or has experience working with dyslexics. Their objective insight can be invaluable to you now and in the future. What we gain and learn about ourselves, especially how to work through the negative effects of dyslexia, can also benefit our dyslexic children.

Leadership is about People and Building Good Relationships

"If you want to build a ship, don't herd people together to collect wood and don't assign them task and work, but rather teach them to long for the endless immensity of the sea."
Antoine de Saint-Exupery, French author and poet

Leadership is the ability to take a vision and then vividly describe that vision to others. It is not the pounding away at the human spirit; it is taking all of the pieces and carefully connecting them together so they work as a whole in pursuit of the open sea.

When you peel away all the buzz terms, leadership is about people and building good, healthy relationships.

I believe dyslexics are often good at leadership because we have to work so hard to achieve what most people take for granted. We understand the jagged edge of the human spirit and how we sometimes have to dig deep to achieve our goals.

Good companies like Virgin Air, The Container Store, or Whole Foods just don't happen overnight. These companies are built on a foundation of good leaders who hire individuals they trust, respect, who share in the leader's vision, and believe in the company's goals. **Leadership requires patience, humility, and faith in another human being.**

Being a good leader also means having confidence in yourself and your team. Most of us have been leading teams since childhood. In school, we often raised our hand first to volunteer when asked to organize or manage teams.

We use our strong visual skills to access quickly all the moving pieces to formulate a plan and then find the best people for each specific part of the process. Think back to when you were in school. How often did you volunteer to lead your study or project group?

Last month, I watched my son Brandon organize a cleanup effort after a band event. He saw what needed to be done and quickly assigned fellow band members to complete the tasks.

One of the greatest competitive advantages for dyslexic entrepreneurs and business owners is when we combine our strong leadership skills with one or a combination of all three entrepreneurial management styles noted in a 2014 Gallup poll study. Leigh Buchman wrote an article for *Inc.* Magazine detailing the results from the study:

- **Activation entrepreneurs are forceful: they make things happen.**
- **Strategic entrepreneurs are big picture thinkers: they are creative and take the long view.**
- **Relational entrepreneurs are highly self-aware: they expand their businesses by building strong relationships.**

What I find interesting about these three types of leadership styles is that dyslexics could be listed in all three categories: from making things happen, to big picture thinking, to building businesses based on trusted relationships. We use this powerful combination of all three styles to launch startups and build strong companies.

Leadership is one of the necessary skills that entrepreneurs must develop to build a successful company. Often times, non-dyslexic founders have little experience or interest in building teams or developing lasting relationships with individuals, which can have negative consequences on the business.

Our strong leadership, interpersonal communication, and team building skills can give us a competitive edge over the competition. All the investors I know fund teams, not ideas. They understand that a startup's products and services will evolve, and the real value of the company is the team. It is important to remember and understand the value you bring to the table.

Remember to never sell yourself short or understate your self-worth.

One final thought about leadership. As team leader, bringing energy to the group is vital. Barbara Corcoran, a dyslexic investor, discussed the importance of having high energy leaders and startup founders in an interview with *Inc.* Magazine. We all love working with people who have positive energy and who have the determination to move past the "no's" and stay focused on the company's vision.

From my experience, creative thinking generates energy. When I have hundreds of thoughts and ideas flowing through my mind or am working on a project I am passionate about, I have endless amounts of energy. Remember, our teams feed off this high positive energy, especially when it is authentic and genuine.

Our Ability to Delegate is a Competitive Edge

"Focus on your strengths and delegate!"
My quote.

The ability to delegate is a major advantage for dyslexic entrepreneurs and professionals. To manage our school work, we learned early how to delegate and build teams. Every dyslexic I interviewed mentioned delegating tasks to mitigate their weaknesses.

Most of us find family and friends to help with non-work related tasks. In school we formed teams and/or delegated homework tasks to our study buddies.

Dr. Logan's research found that "entrepreneurs with dyslexia were more likely to say they were very good at delegation than entrepreneurs who were not dyslexic." Her 2009 study indicated that because we have to delegate more, we place a higher value on our teams. We learned in school that delegating to the right people and building effective teams is vital to our success.

Having strong delegation skills gives dyslexic entrepreneurs a head start over non-dyslexic founders. Dr. Logan also noted that dyslexics tend to grow their companies faster.

Dr. Logan's findings are not surprising. During my interviews for this book, the common theme was that for most of us, delegating is part of life. Several individuals mentioned how they have built informal teams to help read documents and take notes during meetings. Even for this book, I hired editors and asked family and friends to review the manuscript. In conjunction with our ability to delegate, I also believe we are good at networking because our dyslexic brain is constantly seeking potential resources.

Our ability to see the big picture gives us an advantage when we need to find the right person for the job or task. Jim Collins wrote about how good leaders can become great in his book, *Good to Great*. From his research, he noted that great leaders make sure they have the right people in the right places. Aimee Gordon said that her career success in sales was related to her strong leadership ability to delegate and find the right people for each project.

Barbara Corcoran, a dyslexic investor, coaches the startups that she invests in to delegate and hand off tasks they hate. Find people who love to do accounting, finance, operations, and marketing. Align the team members with the jobs they love to do. Barbara delegates the tasks she does not like because she knows that anyone will be better at those tasks than she would be. In an interview with *Inc.* Magazine she stated that there are only two parts of a company the founder or president cannot delegate: judgment and responsibility for the employees.

With my visualization skills, I can see multiple steps ahead when I am problem solving or thinking through a project. While I am processing the information, I quickly determine which part of the process or solution needs to be delegated and then mentally search through my contacts for people who can help. This process is done at an amazing speed as I mentally put the jigsaw pieces together.

Delegation is the art of finding the person that best fits the task or position. It is a learned skill. A dyslexic entrepreneur's success is derived from his or her gut intuition, finding trusted team members who understand their vision, and knowing which individuals should perform which duties.

For dyslexic startups and entrepreneurs, the ability to delegate is a significant competitive advantage.

The Power of Listening

"Having grown up with dyslexia I learned very early in life that if I wanted to take anything in then I had to force myself to listen intently."
Richard Branson

Listening carefully and developing a photographic memory is how I survived school. I still use these skills today. Richard Branson discussed the importance of listening in his book, *The Virgin Way: Everything I Know About Leadership.*

Branson believes that it's not just hearing what the person is saying, but having the ability to truly listen to people. He is concerned that as a society, we are losing this important skill. Listening requires discipline and the ability to focus on the other person instead of thinking about your response or being judgmental.

Most of us relied on our ability to listen intently to our teachers and memorize information that was taught in school. Because of my dysgraphia, I took few class notes. My dyslexic brain instead focused on strengthening my listening and visual processing skills. Even today, I rarely take notes during meetings and focus all my mental energy on listening to the person who is talking. My brain captures the information and details. I use a journal to write key words, short comments, or draw pictures that capture the gist of the conversation or meeting. Another benefit to listening is when you are able to watch the person's facial expressions and other non-verbal cues, which may be just as important. Strong listening skills can give us an advantage during business meetings involving complex matters, such as negotiating a new contract or investor deal. There are times when what is not said in a meeting will have more value than the spoken words.

Listening provides information, especially when meeting new people or joining a group. I have found that when I sit back, watch the interactions, and listen to the group, I can see the informal relationships and group patterns. When we listen to what our teams, customers, and clients are saying, we gain valuable information.

We can miss this information if we focus too much on our devices or how we will respond. Many times our initial questions are answered if we listen to what is being said during the conversation. When we combine our strong listening skills with our gut intuition, we have a powerful asset.

The Brilliance of Visual and Big Picture Thinking

"Seeing the big picture is fast becoming a
killer app in business."
Daniel Pink, A Whole New Mind

Visual or big picture thinking was consistently mentioned by everyone I interviewed and has been noted in the majority of the articles written about dyslexia. Most of us are visual learners and think in images similar to music videos or short movies. Thousands of images are created during our thinking process.

Skip Howard, a dyslexic entrepreneur and inventor, and I were talking about how dyslexia provides a unique ability to see patterns and how trends will evolve in the future. Albert Einstein used his dyslexia to see equations, which enabled him to solve complex mathematical problems. Eric McGehearty, founder and CEO of Globerunner.com, uses his dyslexia talents as an advantage to quickly identify algorithm patterns, which is a huge benefit to his company's SEO (Search Engine Optimization) clients.

I spoke with Lauren Ward who worked as a strategist for several Fortune 500 companies and later started her own consulting firm. Lauren calls herself an "idea strategy person." Her expertise is providing companies with a dyslexic bird's-eye view of the client's business and/or marketing initiatives.

Lauren's insight is unique and an invaluable asset to her clients. She learned how to use dyslexia to her advantage by offering strategic services rather than the execution of the strategy. Her clients value her talent, and the arrangement she creates works well for the whole team.

While working at Bustin & Co., I was a business development manager responsible for helping Nextel Communications expand into new markets. The company hired Bustin to accelerate their business. The client's marketing department and several of our team members were initially pursuing a market segment that did not align with the service Nextel was selling.

For several weeks I thought about the big picture and then pitched a case study idea that would showcase the value of Nextel's new service. The case study became the benchmark for Bustin and Nextel in multiple markets and converted Texas' largest construction company to Nextel's service. The ability to see the whole picture and to understand the whole problem, not just the business side of the matter, but how it impacts everyone, enables us to find the right solution.

Putting the Jigsaw Pieces Together

Considering starting a business? Are you a new entrepreneur? Search for patterns or hidden opportunities competitors might be missing? John Chambers, CEO of Cisco Systems, talked about the advantages of dyslexia and how he pulled information from different data points to create the big picture.

Business Insider interviewed Chambers about being a dyslexic CEO. He stated, "What Dyslexia forces you to do, you don't go from A, B, C, D, E...to Z. I can go A, B ...Z with speed. Because of my weakness I've learned other ways to accomplish the same goal with faster speed. It's easy for me to see how a business proposition is going to play out, or who our next-generation competitors are, from taking this data point from this customer and another data point from another customer and then jump to Z. So it's definitely an advantage."

The speed of seeing the big picture and information patterns is a benefit of dyslexia. Our dyslexic brains developed finely tuned neurons, unique pathways, and shortcuts to visually process information at an amazing speed.

We developed this skill to survive school when we had to absorb significant amounts of information and then quickly distill the information to find the main point.

Remember, as visionary big picture thinkers, it is important to delegate to team members who excel at tactical execution and enjoy the role.

Big Data Curation

We are experiencing a digital transformation which is changing and disrupting many industries. Strategies and processes that worked in the past are quickly becoming obsolete. Thomas West, a dyslexic professor and author, wrote about how our unique ability to see the big picture and to visually process data will increase in demand as our world becomes driven by big data.

With the flood of big data, companies are seeking a way to curate and understand the information. Daniel Pink wrote about the importance of big picture thinking in his book *A Whole New Mind*. He stated, "A world teeming with information, individual choices, and just plain stuff is putting a premium on this aptitude [big picture thinking] in our personal lives as well. Modern life's glut of options and stimuli can be so overwhelming that those with the ability to see the big picture – to sort out what really matters – have a decided advantage in their pursuit of personal well-being."

Dyslexics have the ability to sort out what matters. Our gift is the ability to quickly process information and get to the root of the problem. The demand for companies and professionals who can understand and distill big data into meaningful relationships will grow in demand as our consumption of big data increases.

Many companies are still unsure exactly how to use all the data they receive from social media networks, website analytics, and customer clicks. The human element is still required to interpret and determine the real story buried in the data.

Dyslexic business owners and professionals who can curate big data, find meaningful relationships, and then develop a strategy from the data will have a significant advantage.

Distill Ideas to the Core

In general, dyslexics seem to have an innate ability to drill down to the point and understand a problem or idea at its core. Earlier this month a former business partner was talking about his startup and social app. I quickly could see how the app would work and what market opportunities he had missed.

I kept saying, *"I get it!"* But he kept on talking until I drew a picture of my interpretation of his concept and what I envisioned as the target market for the product. He was amazed at my insight and how quickly I grasped the gist of his concept.

We learned in school to get to the heart of the matter and toss unnecessary information to the side in order to find the fastest path to a solution. Dyslexic entrepreneurs and startups can have an advantage in the market place by quickly distilling market trends and building products before competitors see the opportunity. Everyone I talked with for this book mentioned distilling ideas to their core as a key strength.

Aimee Gordon talked about her ability to summarize a complex matter to its simplest form as a valuable asset. Simplifying an idea is harder than creating a complex system that is hard to use. Digging through the details is laborious and our brain finds the fastest route to the answer using visual processing skills. While I was visiting with Aimee Gordon and Lauren Ward, we all discussed how that once we distilled the problem and devised a strategic plan, we were ready to take action!

Industries and professions that can be automated will most likely be managed by computers or robots in the near future. Dyslexic entrepreneurs and business owners with strong big picture thinking skills and the ability to condense large amounts of data for their clients will have a competitive edge over their competition.

In a world of abundance, businesses and individuals will need companies and services that can distill our overwhelming number of choices into meaningful information.

Thoughts to Consider:
- Find ways to maximize your big picture thinking skills and incorporate this strength into your business or corporate position.
- Often times the advantages of dyslexia have become so ingrained in our brains we have forgotten these skills are an asset which can be used for our benefit.
- Think about how you can use this strength as an asset.

- Is there a position at your company that would align your big picture thinking skills?
- Remember to search for opportunities to use your big picture thinking strengths in your business or career.

Your Visualization Skills Can Be a Competitive Advantage

"From the time dyslexics entered kindergarten, they've had to solve their own problems."
Seth Goldman, co-founder of Honest Tea

During my conversation with Skip Howard, a dyslexic entrepreneur and inventor, I asked him to describe how he solved problems. He used a story to explain how he developed a new software program in college. This program was one of his first major successes. I had a light bulb moment while listening to Skip as I realized dyslexics often times use stories to solve problems.

Skip's software program was designed to help reduce the stress of university counselors. The counselors were spending hours following up with students who had disciplinary actions or other problems that needed immediate attention by the student so they could stay enrolled or receive their diploma. Skip said, "I wanted to understand the whole process, not just a single pain point. So, I interviewed counselors to obtain a deeper understanding of why they were using the current process, what tasks they did on a daily basis, and their job requirements. I wanted to know what the real purpose was for what they were doing."

When the software program was completed and tested at the university, the counselors could not believe how much the program changed their work and life. Gone were the long additional hours spent performing redundant tasks. Secondly, the old process and system created work scope creep, which means the counselors were assigned new responsibilities outside their defined work position. These added responsibilities created more stress. Their job had changed from being a guidance career counselor to a paralegal position, which added another layer of stress for the counselors.

Skip still remembers how one counselor starting crying with joy and kept saying, "You do not know how much this means to us." Our ability to connect with people and listen to their stories enables us to obtain a whole picture view of all the moving pieces related to the problem. Understanding what is at the heart of the problem is crucial.

Also understanding why the problem is occurring, not just from one angle, but from all the angles, enables us to find a solution that will work.

Our 30,000 Foot View

Dyslexics see the forest, the trees, which trees are growing, which trees are fading, and everything in between.

From visiting with fellow dyslexics, I can see how we all have our own style of problem solving. However, there is a dyslexia theme that is consistent in each of us. By visualizing the whole picture, we are able to mentally put the jigsaw pieces together.

I can't imagine not having the ability to visually solve problems. I use my visual processing and problem solving skills constantly to find solutions at work and at home. My dyslexic brain functions like a Rubik's cube, where you mentally go through all of the possibilities to quickly find an answer.

During my conversation with Seth Goldman, co-founder of Honest Tea, he mentioned that dyslexics have been solving problems from day one. He went on to say that finding our own solutions and solving problems is very natural to us. Learning how to solve complex problems in school was stated in multiple articles as the reason why so many dyslexics are business owners or entrepreneurs.

I believe the greatest value of our dyslexic brain is the ability to quickly find a work around or solution.

Goldman went on to say that we are comfortable at solving our own problems and achieving our goals many do not believe we can accomplish. I also believe that our brain thrives on the challenge of solving complex problems as most of us become bored when our brain is idle.

As visual problem solvers, our ability to turn the problem upside down, inside out, and view from a completely different angle can provide insight to formulating a solution. We daydream about a solution or think of an alternative way to work through a problem by swapping out different elements that may or may not work. **The dyslexic brain loves patterns. It feasts upon information with a goal of finding a solution.** At times when we are solving problems, it appears to the outside world that we are doing nothing. Staring into space, we mentally process information in a random fashion to find an answer.

When I was in graduate school, I solved a problem very differently than my classmates. The professor marked the problem wrong even though I had the correct answer. I was proud that I found a different way to solve the problem and discussed the matter with my tutor, who was also a professor. She explained with humor that accounting is not the best discipline for creative problem solving. Operation management classes were more rewarding because I loved the mental challenge of eliminating bottlenecks.

All my life I have used my strong visualization skills to solve problems, from finding the fast path, to learning new material at school, to assessing a business problem for a client. Many times this process is done while I am running for exercise, as I can visualize different projects and what needs to be done. I believe our ability to use our visual thinking and find the whole story behind the problem is a competitive edge.

As our world continues to change, our visual problem solving skills and talents will be in demand and increase in value.

Along with our problem solving abilities, we have the ability to quickly distill complex ideas and concepts. This gift of simplifying large volumes of information is derived from our ability to see the problem visually and then cut to the heart of the matter. Aimee Gordon talked about her ability to summarize a complex matter to its simplest form as a valuable asset. Digging through the details is laborious, and our brain finds the fastest route to the answer using visual processing skills.

Our ability to solve problems was mentioned in every conversation I had while writing this book and is considered one of the most valuable assets of dyslexia. Our digital transformation is changing how we work, live, and interact with our family and friends.

Dyslexics have more opportunities today than ever before to showcase the brilliance of the dyslexic brain and its ability to solve complex problems with amazing speed.

Capitalize on Your Verbal Communication Strengths

"As a kid, I learned quickly how to capitalize on my verbal communication skills to compensate for my weaknesses in writing and reading."
My quote.

Dyslexics are often vivid story-tellers. We use our verbal communication skills during business meetings to describe our vision. I can convey my thoughts faster verbally than writing them down, and often times I talk by phone or meet in person to discuss my idea.

While writing this book, I read the manuscript out loud and verbally discussed my thoughts before I wrote the words. Starting in childhood, dyslexics rely heavily on their verbal communication skills to help compensate for their weaknesses in writing, reading, and spelling.

Pat Ryan, a retired dyslexic entrepreneur and business owner, stated that his ability to communicate with people was one of the key reasons for his success. Several of my dyslexic friends are successful sales executives who use their strong communication and storytelling skills to their advantage.

People remember a good story. When someone tells us a story, often times we remember the details more than a presentation full of bullet points. Chip Heath and Dan Heath wrote about the power of stories in their best-selling book *Made to Stick,* which I recommend reading.

Tell Us a Story

From the beginning of humanity, we have used stories to explain our history and passed down knowledge to the next generation. Using our strong verbal skills, we can engage and connect with our audiences. Companies and businesses know today that connecting with their customers through powerful online stories is a necessity. To rise above the noise on the Internet, businesses, employees, and professionals must have an authentic story.

Many dyslexics select a career in sales so they can fully utilize their strong verbal communication skills and storytelling abilities to build long-term relationships with customers. Telling a good story requires a vivid imagination mixed with creativity and empathy.

One key thing to remember is that your idea must be solid and memorable. When constructing your sales or elevator pitch, think of how you can make your story stick.

Distill the idea to its core and find one or two memorable aspects that will resonate with the customer, client, or investor.

- In a flurry of ideas, what part of the idea rises to the top?
- Think about the staying power of the story. Can your story adapt to our changing business environment?

With the rapid increase of viewership on YouTube, everyone, including me, is working to capitalize on this trend. I love the power of digital videos. There are hundreds of individuals making six figure incomes by posting daily videos to YouTube.

Dyslexics can use digital videos to their advantage since we can verbally paint a picture faster than writing and editing a blog post or article. With the advancement of video communication, it is easier now than ever before to create internal videos for sharing ideas. Viewing digital content on our devices is rapidly increasing and will continue to evolve.

Thoughts to Consider:
- Are you fully utilizing your verbal communication and storytelling skills?
- Can your business benefit from using digital videos to promote your story and engage with existing or potential new customers?
- Do you notice new trends evolving from digital video and media that your business could use as an advantage?

- Same for professionals – can you maximize your storytelling abilities to strengthen your sales or business development presentations?
- Can you replace written memos with videos? Using the iPhone iMovie app, you can create a video, edit, and add voice-over comments. My prediction for the future is Digital Video Memos.
- Can you and your team benefit from informal stand-up meetings for quick updates?

Maximizing Your Verbal Strengths

Using our strong verbal skills to our advantage can benefit our businesses and professional careers. It is important to focus on your communication strengths. If you excel in small team communication, find ways to use this asset to your advantage.

Conversely, if you enjoy public speaking, seek out opportunities to speak more often. An interesting note from my interviews: about half of the group I spoke with preferred small group communication and the other half enjoyed public speaking.

Learning to recognize and maximize your communication strength is the best strategy.

We are very good at talking on our feet, and many of us have chosen professions where we use our strong verbal skills to our advantage. I started in sales and am now a professional speaker. In college I joined Toastmasters International, which gave me the opportunity to strengthen my verbal skills. In addition to Toastmasters, there are public speaking and sales groups listed on Meetup.com. You can search by zip code and find groups in your area that are related to speaking and/or to your profession.

Our verbal communication skills are a prized trait and it is the deciding factor between securing a new project or a new employment position. It is important to find avenues that you can use to maintain your strong verbal skills.

Dyslexic startups and entrepreneurs who can succinctly communicate their vision to investors will have a better chance of securing funding. Today, dyslexics have more opportunities to capitalize on their strong verbal communication skills than previous in generations.

Strategies for When Your Word Retrieval System Misfires

"My word retrieval system has misfired."
Brandon Belanger, teen business owner and founder of
Urban Art 12

As a rule, we are more comfortable speaking about our passions and topics we know well. However, sometimes when we are asked to provide a response on the spot, our word retrieval system does not work, and our minds go blank.

When speaking with Aimee Gordon, Ryan Kinzy, and Skip Howard, they all said they have a delay in their response when they receive an on-demand question or are thrown off base by a comment.

While writing this book, I learned about on-demand questions and how small talk can be potentially tricky for dyslexics. For example, I was recently at an event at my son's school after a long work week, and my dyslexic brain's word retrieval system was not working well.

When several parents asked me questions, I noticed that my response time was very slow and the wrong words were coming out of my mouth. I finally said to one parent, "I'm dyslexic and my word retrieval system is not working." She gave me a strange look and said "Okay." Later in the evening, when another parent asked about my business, the conversation went smoother.

Dr. Shaywitz wrote about delays in our verbal responses in her book *Overcoming Dyslexia.* Her explanation made sense, and now I understand why the dyslexic brain can have communication misfires. She stated that for dyslexics, providing an oral response "on the spot is slow and labored." She explained why there are times when we speak backwards or invert our words. This also explains why we were slow to respond to our teachers when called upon in class. I remember classmates making fun of my slow response or incorrect words when my word retrieval system was out of whack.

Dr. Shaywitz discussed our reliance on words such as "like," "stuff," "you know", and my favorite word, "thingy", when we are attempting to respond. Many times when we are asked a specific question in a social setting, our dyslexic brain can be on a different intellectual plane, which can cause a delay in our response as well.

Gaining this awareness and knowledge allows us the opportunity to create a plan that will help reduce our communication misfires. I have been thinking of solutions on how to better manage small talk and on-demand responses at social events or when I am mentally tired. I think it is important to share these ideas with our dyslexic children as well.

Role playing or thinking of a response to potential questions in advance can help. Another idea is to think about several open-ended questions that you can ask to move a conversation along.

Skip Howard had several great ideas on how to manage small talk. When he is asked a question at his son's school or a social event, he has a list of responses ready. For example, when asked a question he says, "That's a good question, how do you handle it?" or "Tell me more about (fill in the blank)." He works to turn the table back to the other person in the conversation. By listening to conversation, he has time to think of a response. Skip and I discussed how our brains are generally moving at light speed processing a conversation. Often, we become sidetracked because we discover something interesting from the conversation, which generates a magnitude of questions. I have found that flooding a person with questions during small talk does not work well.

Another strategy I use for social events and business meetings is to review LinkedIn or Facebook before the event. When I arrive at the event, I have a couple of small talk topics in my back pocket to start the conversation, and then like Skip, I redirect the conversation back to the individual or group. Finally, when I am mentally tired and know I'm not at my best, I am polite but keep small talk to a minimum.

One of my favorite books is Stephen Covey's *The 7 Habits of Highly Effective People*. In the book he discusses how we have the ability to determine our reaction between the stimulus (what was asked or said to us) and our response. Reading Covey's book was helpful, as the information was a good reminder to pause and allow our brain time to mentally shift gears.

This brief mental regroup allows us the opportunity to think about the question and the words we need to retrieve. **Having a tool box of dyslexia strategies is important when managing our sometimes non-functioning word retrieval system.**

Connecting the Dots –
The Dyslexic Network

"You can't connect the dots looking forward; you can only connect them looking backwards. So you have to trust that the dots will somehow connect in your future."
Steve Jobs, Stanford Commencement Address, 2005

Our ability to build extensive professional networks is an added benefit. Since junior high, I've always been curious about meeting people and learning something new. Several of the dyslexic sales directors I interviewed for the book talked about how they spend time building personal connections and focus on developing long-term relationships.

Our networks provide support and references for services that we may need in the future.

Another advantage that dyslexia provides is the ability to see patterns in unrelated connections that our non-dyslexic peers may miss. As I wrote earlier, we are often times gifted at seeing patterns and can find trends from unrelated data. When I attend networking events, my dyslexic brain will scan subconsciously for ways to connect relationships with business projects or search for new trends. I have found that when I meet people, the connection may not always be evident; however, later I can see how the connections match.

For example, last year when I started writing *You Posted What!?*, several unrelated connections that I made years ago proved to be invaluable to me as a new author. Two individuals edited the manuscript and a couple of others participated in the crowd-funding campaign. I have a gut feeling when I meet new people. Steve Jobs summed connecting the dots best during his 2005 Stanford Commencement Address. One of Jobs' quotes from his presentation was mentioned under the section title.

Our personal networks and connections are stored in our minds or written on scraps of paper and sticky notes in our offices. Yet, we remember in detail how and why the connection matters. Our networks are evolving as we connect with individuals around the world.

Social media is a good tool for building relationships outside your local area. However, I believe that the old-school way of one-on-one meetings and telephone conversations still have value. Finding a way to manage contact information is important as our networks increase in size and expand around the globe.

I currently use Highrise and Google Apps to manage contact information for both my business and personal networks. Even though I use a digital database, I also keep a person's business card and write a few notes on the back of the card for future reference. Many times I can find a person's name quicker looking through the business cards rather than scrolling through names on a screen. My dyslexic brain remembers the whole picture of the person's business card, printed graphics, and my notes.

Our networks are an invaluable asset. I have learned through the years to nurture my business and personal connections by reaching out when I see a post on LinkedIn or invite them to coffee to catch up.

These connections are your lifeline when you need help. And conversely, you are part of their lifeline. Remember to take time to nurture your business and personal relationships.

Dyslexic Career Alignment – Creativity Required!

"Real artists ship."
Steve Jobs

Researchers are still working to nail down why dyslexics are generally more creative than their non-dyslexic peers. From the time we could crawl, our brains have been constantly seeking an outlet for our creative energy. The dyslexic brain is always thinking, moving, processing, and creating.

This can be a bit of an annoyance to our family and friends. In fact, it appears that our brains are hard-wired for creative thinking. In 2013 Melinda Beck wrote an article for *The Wall Street Journal* titled "Dyslexia Workarounds: Creativity Without a Lot of Reading." Her article included information about how MRI images presented real biological evidence that supported studies on why dyslexics are **highly creative, out-of-the-box thinkers, and really do think differently."**

For most of us, having a creative outlet is a must. During my conversation with Ryan Kinzy, we discussed creativity and the need to express our creative energy. He has written several children's books while working as a software developer and project manager. Selecting a profession that provides a creative channel or finding a hobby outside of work is important.

I know from personal experience that if you have no creative outlet at work, then you must find one at home. While working in enforcement for FINRA, I remember thinking that I could not mentally last much longer sitting in a cubicle following a paper trail of a broker committing insider trading. During lunch, I made up stories, which allowed my brain some free recess time to create and daydream. Interestingly, while creating these stories, I linked investigative points together which would later benefit the insider trading case. My dyslexic brain needed its recess time to create and problem solve.

Last year I visited with Andres Traslavina, Global Talent Recruiter for Whole Foods Market, Inc. We connected on LinkedIn and I was curious to learn more about how he placed executives for unique companies, such as Whole Foods. Andres is an experienced recruiter who has worked for multiple Fortune 500 companies. He talked about the importance of making sure we do not place our "ladder" on the wrong wall.

Andres confirmed that individuals who build their education and career around their innate talent are more successful. As a rule, during interviews, Andres seeks an individual who has aligned their innate talents, skills, and experiences. He tends to shy away from candidates who had straight A's and no outside interests or passions.

In the interviews I conducted while writing the book, **everyone mentioned the importance of aligning their dyslexic brain, talents, and creativity with their careers.** I know from experience that combining your experiences, strengths, and dyslexic talents provides the most benefit. My father is a retired CPA. He encouraged me to become an accountant, which is one of the least creative professions a person can select. I worked in several positions that were stressful and did not align my skills and talents.

When I became a business owner, I could finally align my talents and experiences and use my dyslexic brain to my advantage.

Thoughts to Consider:
- If you are currently in a position that does not fulfill your creative needs, think about how you can find a creative outlet to enjoy during your free time.
- For professionals interested in writing, WordPress. org offers a free platform for bloggers and writers.
- Like I mentioned earlier in the Verbal Communication section, search Meetup for groups or activities that can help express your creative energy.
- For professionals who are considering a career change, assess the importance of having a creative outlet in your job. There are startups that focus on matching an individual's talent with the right position and organization. Last year I interviewed

the founders of www.HireArt.com. Their goal was to change how companies and employment candidates find each other.

- **Network and explore new opportunities.** Consider how you can use your creative dyslexic brain, problem solving, and strong communication skills in a different industry or position.
- **Technology is creating new industries**, businesses, and careers that need highly creative, visual thinkers. Working for a startup or a small business often times provides more flexibility to use your dyslexic brain's full potential.

The Elephant in the Room

"Trust Yourself. You know more than you think you do."
Dr. Spock, famous pediatrician in the 1940s

For this book to be complete, I believe a brief discussion about the darker side of dyslexia is important. It is the elephant in the room. Everyone I interviewed talked about how dyslexia impacted their self-confidence as a kid and how they still experience periods of self-doubt when their intelligence is questioned or their word-retrieval system fails.

Each person's self-confidence undulates and is dependent upon internal and external factors. As we mature, we can manage our responses to tacky comments better than when we were kids.

Even when the rational and logical part of my brain tells me to let a tacky comment slide, I would be lying if I said the remarks didn't sting. As an adult, my personal awareness has changed, and I focus on educating individuals about the **value of dyslexia** instead of focusing solely on the weaknesses.

Understanding how our self-confidence and childhood baggage can play a role in our businesses and careers is important. During each interview I conducted, the person's energy level would increase when they discussed their creative pursuits, businesses, or talents.

As dyslexic kids, we found ways to self-motivate and hold our confidence together. I learned early to find subjects, such as math and history, where I could excel and focused on being a top student. Another internal motivator was to find an outlet for my creative energy at home by developing new products to sell at my mother's art gallery or by writing stories. I thought about the future a lot and did not dwell too much on what was happening in the classroom.

I believe most of us never truly lose faith in ourselves even when we feel our self-confidence has reached rock bottom. Through the years, we have developed a way to prevail regardless of the obstacles in front us. While in school, my self-confidence was tested twice, as I mentioned in the Resiliency section. Each time, I found the courage to stand my ground and refused to be discriminated against. **Everyone's confidence is stronger when we pursue a career that aligns with our innate talent, expertise, and experience.**

In Dr. Cloud's book *Integrity* he discussed how people with well-defined identities do well in life. These individuals know what they like, what they don't like, and have healthy boundaries. Dr. Cloud discussed how we know immediately when we meet these individuals, because they know who they are and they have a defined personal mission.

He wrote, "These defined individuals also know exactly what they are good at and what they are not. They live in their areas of strengths and talents and do not spend much time thinking that they are something they are not. In that way, not only do they work hard, but when they are working, they are working on things that have a chance of succeeding."

Dyslexics wrote the book on pivoting, adjusting, tweaking, and doing whatever it took to make it through school and then building a solid career or business.

We learned in elementary school that life doesn't give you bumpers to keep everything in a neat, pretty row. I believe as we continue to discover the true value of dyslexia, and focus on the brilliance of the dyslexic brain, we will focus less on its weaknesses.

Project and Time Management Strategies and Tools

"Things which matter most must never be at the mercy of things which matter least."
Goethe, famous philosopher

Time is our most valuable asset, and developing a management system that is realistic and works with your dyslexic brain is important. I have developed a system which works well with my business and personal schedules; it is a blend of technology and old school.

There are thousands of books on time management and making your team more productive. However, I have learned that for time management system to work it must make sense, be simple, and effective. Adding another program or process generally does not increase productivity.

Often times, teams can benefit from the reduction of steps or the elimination of a process.

Sometimes we allow others to steer us off course or lose sight of our original vision or goal. I recently read Peter Ducker's book *The Effective Executive*, which made me rethink how I spend my time. Being busy and slammed at the office is not new. Ever since the clock was invented, humans have wrestled with time management.

What I learned from Ducker is to eliminate multitasking, that doing too many tasks at once does not save time in the long run. Now I set aside time to complete complex tasks that require my full attention. For example, while writing this book, I turned off all notifications, emails, and did not answer my phone. Having quiet time was invaluable so I could focus my attention on completing the manuscript without interruptions.

Another strategy I use is to "**eat the frog**," which is part of a famous phrase written by Mark Twain. His message encouraged individuals to complete difficult tasks in the morning rather than procrastinating until later. This is important for new business owners, since delaying a task or project can impede the growth of the business.

When you find yourself procrastinating, make a decision: eliminate the task, delegate it to someone else, or "eat the frog!"

Spending your time on the right tasks and projects is important. To prepare for 2015, I worked with my business advisors and team to review our current business activities and new projects. We listed our needs, goals, and where we would spend our time and resources. Out-of-date business functions, "time-sucks", and other non-essential business activities were eliminated. As a business owner, single parent, and author, I do not like spending time or resources on activities that do not benefit my business or have a meaningful purpose.

Business meetings and being glued to social media updates may be other areas where your time is wasted away. Before scheduling a meeting, confirm with your team that there is a defined purpose or reason to meet. Another idea is to schedule 15 minute stand-up meetings for project updates or status reports.

Make sure the team understands why the meeting has been scheduled and what action items will be discussed. Use your ability to distill the problem or project to determine the purpose of the meeting and what needs to be completed. Find ways to streamline or eliminate traditional office processes that have little or no benefit. Think creatively about how to use your time effectively and with a purpose.

It is important to understanding how, where, and why you spend time on projects and tasks. Gaining an insight as to why you are doing something will enable you to make adjustments or eliminate the project altogether. For creative dyslexics, scheduling time to think, invent, and create is important; it is part of the process of developing new concepts and solving complex problems.

In the following section, I have listed digital tools, software programs, and products that I use to manage my business.

Project and Time Management Tools

Basecamp (formally 37 Signals)

I have used Basecamp for project management and business development for almost seven years and love the simplicity of the application. What I like best about Basecamp is that I can store information that I do not want to forget.

When I am conducting research on the Internet and find an article that is related to a new book that I am writing or project, I copy and paste the link to a file in Basecamp. By doing this, I do not have numerous tabs open in Google Chrome. I mentally know the links are saved and can review them at a later time. Each month, I go through and clean out the article links I no longer need. www.basecamp.com

Highrise

Highrise is a contact manager for small businesses, which was originally created by Basecamp. I previously used Microsoft Office to my manage business and personal contacts. There are new software applications launched each year to help manage our digital networks.

I have found that selecting a contact management system or program that is easy to use and works well for the entire team provides the most benefit. www.highrise.com

Dropbox

Gone are the days of having to zip a large file. We use Dropbox to share files and videos sharing with clients and vendors. I also use Google Drive for storing and sharing files. Again, find a program that works best for your business, employees, and clients. www.dropbox.com

Tools to For Capturing Your Creative Energy

Thomas Edison and Leonardo da Vinci had hundreds of journals in which they wrote down ideas and captured their thoughts. Two years ago I met Brandon Oldenburg who won an Oscar for Best Animated Short Film. He mentioned that the idea for the film was ten years in the making. The original idea for the movie occurred in college, and he mentally worked on the script until it finally became a film.

Journals

Sometimes, finding a way to harness our creative energy can be difficult and laborious, especially when our dyslexic brain is in full gear. Five years ago I started using a journal to capture my ideas and drawings. Previously, my ideas were written on sticky notes, backs of envelopes, or whatever piece of paper was on my desk. At first it felt like the journal restrained my creativity, but after a while, I adapted to capturing my ideas in one location. I tape images from magazines and articles in my journals to help visually recreate an idea. I have discovered that keeping a journal helps ground my dyslexic brain. Having my thoughts collected in one location has been beneficial, since I can look back and see the evolution of my thought process.

My favorite journals are Moleskine. I have multiple journals which are color coded with a specific purpose. I also use different colored Sharpies to write notes, draw ideas, and separate the different lines of thought. www.moleskine.com

Whiteboards

My house is filled with whiteboards, in my office, in Brandon's room, and the kitchen. We use different colored markers to differentiate our schedules, action items, and creative thoughts. I have trained my brain to know the specific action items by color so that when I look at the whiteboard, I can quickly identify the action item or task. For example, we use the color blue for scheduled meetings, green for business development projects, and red for urgent.

Jumbo Easel Pad Sticky Notes

I love jumbo easel pad sticky notes for brainstorming meetings, drafting project outlines and for capturing ideas. These large sticky notes can be kept for future reference. Staying with the color coding theme, we use different colored Sharpies to separate lines of thinking and to link different strategies.

Evernote

Evernote is another good tech tool for saving creative thoughts and information. I am still learning Evernote and thinking through how I can use the application. For now, Basecamp is the primary program we use for all three businesses. So far, what I like best about Evernote are virtual sticky notes and how you can add photos to your grocery list. www.evernote.com

Organizing Systems

Staying organized and curating all our digital data can feel overwhelming. Technology is great. However, my dyslexic brain still prefers pencil and paper. The printed articles feel more concrete in my mind, and I can write notes in the margin for future reference.

Our office file folders are colored-coded for a quick reference, too. The same colors are used for consistently so I can quickly view our whiteboards, jumbo sticky notes, or files to find the information I am seeking.

Calendars

About half of the dyslexic entrepreneurs who helped with this book use digital calendars, whereas the other half uses paper calendars. Aimee Gordon and I discussed how we have to write down our notes and to-dos or the information will not become concrete in our dyslexic brains. I have difficulty keeping the time zones correct when scheduling calls to the East or West Coast.

When I recently scheduled a telephone meeting for 11:00 A.M. central (in my mind), the person was thinking 11:00 A.M. eastern. I missed our initial call but was able to connect later with the person. I feel more organized when I write down on paper and on the office whiteboard my schedule and action items.

Sometimes my mind becomes mentally jumbled when reading addresses or action items on a computer screen or my iPhone. I have a tendency to reverse or misread dates or addresses.

Spiral Notebook

I use a spiral notebook as my daily calendar. For me, writing down the action items and making notes is the best way to organize my day. Each day I write the date and then list four or five action items I want to complete. Backburner items are stored on Basecamp and creative thoughts are written in my journal.

For critical tasks, I highlight in yellow to remind me that I must complete the task. The organization system I use is a modification of the system I developed in high school and have found that a combination of online software, digital technology, and "old school paper" works best for me.

Remember the most efficient strategy for managing projects and your schedule is to create a system that works well with your management style and your dyslexia.

The Importance of Exercising

"I was living to run and running to live."
Bob Seger, musician and singer *"Against the Wind"*

I started running for exercise eleven years ago. At first, I ran two to three miles a week. Gradually, I increased my mileage. To date, I have completed multiple 5Ks, a half, and a full marathon. Each week I run between 15 – 25 miles, depending on my work schedule.

As a runner, I have transitioned to where I run more to think during the "alone time" than for staying healthy or preparing for a race. I have discovered that running four to five times a week centers my high-energy, dyslexic brain.

Running provides the opportunity to mentally chew on problems, think of new ideas, and see the big picture without interruption. I run without my iPhone and listen to the rhythm of my pounding shoes on the pavement.

I am not a scientist or a doctor, but I believe the rhythmic movement helps the dyslexic brain, plus running provides quiet time to think and process. I believe exercise is very important for everyone, especially business owners and professionals who work long hours and/or travel extensively. **Exercise is a must-do on our schedule and not a backburner item.** Some individuals have found getting up early and excising before their day starts works best, while others prefer to exercise after work. **Find a time and create a schedule that works for you.** James Carville, a well-known political advisor, mentioned in an interview with *Runner's* Magazine that he carries a pair of running shoes everywhere he goes. During Clinton's presidential campaign Carville often ran in hotel lobbies. Maybe that is why I like running. It is easy to do and easy to fit into my schedule.

Richard Branson wrote about the importance of exercising and staying healthy in his book *Like a Virgin: Secrets They Don't Teach You In Business School.* He discussed the importance of taking time off from work to swim, run, or play sports as this downtime allows your brain to relax and recharge.

Brad Feld, a well known entrepreneur and venture capitalist, wrote about the importance of exercise, healthy eating, and finding a balance. For me, running four to five times a week provides a huge benefit mentally and physically.

If running doesn't work for you, find another outlet and make it a priority!

Digital Technology is Creating a Level Playing Field

"Technology is dyslexia's ramp."
Ellen O'Neill, Executive Director for the Atlantic
Seaboard Dyslexia Education Center

Bill Gates and Steve Jobs profoundly changed the world, especially for dyslexics. With the introduction of Microsoft Office, checking our written work became as easy as clicking a button.

Gone were the days of having to retype and "white out" misspelled words. It is truly amazing how much the world has changed. Now, technology is interwoven into every part of our lives. In the future, digital technology will mitigate many of the problems we encounter related to reading, spelling, or writing.

Each month I read in *Wired* Magazine or in the *Tech Crunch* RSS feed about a new program or mobile app developed for dyslexics.

My son has difficulty spelling and uses his iPhone to obtain the correct spelling: he asks Siri how to spell the word. He uses the voice dedication function to dictate his text messages and emails.

Eric McGehearty, a dyslexic CEO, uses technology extensively to mitigate his dyslexia. He dictates his emails and uses an audio reading program which converts documents, files, messages, and into spoken words. To avoid distracting employees, Eric wears one of his ear buds to listen while the others read.

While writing this book, my iPhone was invaluable tool for spell check and finding the right word. If Siri could not find the correct spelling, I used Google Search. From my experience, using the misspelled word in a sentence helps Google Analytics locate the correct word faster. I also use the Merrian-Webster iPhone app when I need to hear how a word sounds or to look up a word's definition. There are times when I will type a word and it is incorrect, but I cannot see the mistake.

Earlier this year I visited with Ellen O'Neill, who is the Executive Director for the Atlantic Seaboard Dyslexia Education Center. We discussed how technology is creating a whole new world for dyslexics. The analogy she used to explain how technology will benefit dyslexic individuals is similar to how the wheelchair ramp provided greater accessibility to individuals who were wheelchair bound.

Ellen stated, "We do not notice these ramps anymore because we use the ramps without much thought." Technology will be our ramp as it will increase our opportunities and provide a more level playing field.

Digital technology and the Internet will be a pivotal game changer for dyslexics. I exchanged emails with Lars Bo Nielsen, an export manager for MV-Nordic, a company based in Denmark which has created a new app that can be downloaded to your device.

Using the app, you select content either in an email or on a website and the app will convert the text to audio. Like I have said before, this is just the tip of the iceberg. I cannot wait to see what new technology programs and apps will be developed for dyslexics this year.

The Stewardship of Dyslexic Students

"If your dreams don't scare you, they are too small."
Richard Branson

Dreams and goals are critical to encouraging and empowering dyslexic students. As I mentioned in the Dream Big or Go Home! section of this book, there are still individuals who seek to squash our children's dreams rather than encourage them to explore new opportunities.

Several educators I spoke with in the United States and the United Kingdom stressed the need for good role models. We can help the next generation of dyslexics by finding time in our schedules to speak at our local schools.

To these young adults, we are all rock stars. Hearing how we use dyslexia to our advantage can make all the difference in the world. When I was speaking at my son's junior high school recently, I mentioned that I was dyslexic. A student immediately said, "I am, too!" and smiled.

She was so excited to hear that she was not alone, and the look on her face was priceless.

With the increased focus on STEM (Science, Technology, Engineering and Math), it is important to ensure all students have a creative outlet. The University of Texas at Dallas has created an ATEC program combining art and technology which I believe is a great idea. Dyslexic students need a creative outlet to allow their imagination time to think and create.

By reaching out to students, we can offer encouragement and guidance on how to align their dyslexic talents, strengths, skills, and passions.

I did not learn about successful dyslexics until I reached college age, and most of the time the list of dyslexics was short, including only five or six actors, scientists, and business owners. Our community of dyslexic role models is growing, and it is important to help support the next generation of dyslexic business owners and professionals.

Following the publication of this book, I plan to write and publish a book for teens. The working title is *Dyslexic Teens – How to Start a Business or Launch a Career before High School Graduation.*

Celebrate the Next Generation of Dyslexic Entrepreneurs

"Dyslexics can transverse across multiple mediums and see a totally new interpretation that becomes the basis for an innovative idea."
My quote.

Young dyslexic entrepreneurs are blazing new trails by creating apps, programs, and starting their own businesses early. Many of these founders are creating products that solve pain points they encountered in school. The Internet has greatly reduced the barriers of entry for starting a business.

College-age dyslexics and teens are using their creative minds to develop their ideas into viable businesses. My son, Brandon started his first business when he was 10. He is the founder and owner of Urban Art 12 – an urban design business. His products are sold online and at a local farmer's market.

Every aspect of how we work, live, and interact with our customers, clients, peers, and co-workers is changing. In *You Posted What!?* I wrote about how technology is changing every part of our world, from employment to how we manage our personal affairs. Even our physical offices are changing.

When someone asks where my company is based I say, "the cloud", because the Internet is an integral part of my business. Daniel Pink wrote about how corporate America was evolving in his book *Free Agent Nation* and stated, "Power is devolving from the organization to the individual. The individual, not the organization, has become the economy's fundamental unit." Companies that understand this change will have an advantage in the new economy.

For example, **Adam Neumann** is co-founder of WeWork Companies a four-year-old startup that provides office space to startups. The company is capitalizing on this new trend by offering office sharing space that fulfills the needs of micro businesses. Neumann discussed the goals for WeWork in *The Wall Street Journal* article by Lindsay Gellman and Eliot Brown.

Neumann stated that he "hopes to make the company a hothouse for new business formation – by bringing together entrepreneurs who share space, office services and, potentially, ideas." Being a dyslexic entrepreneur, Neumann understands how startups and micro businesses need a place to work, collaborate, and socialize.

Remind is another startup co-founded by Brett and David Kopf. The brothers wanted to create a safe way for teachers to communicate with students and parents. Brett is dyslexic and is open about why he and his brother created Remind. Brett's advice for building a company is to "build a simple product, talk to your users, and solve someone's problem."

The brothers understood the value of finding good mentors early to help them during the product development phase. Brett mentioned how the guidance gained from their mentors was invaluable. Remind has received funding and support from imagek12 – an edtech accelerator.

Gary Smith is founder of Brainbook Ltd., and creator of the Dyslexia Toolbox. The company is based in the United Kingdom. Gary created the Dyslexia Toolbox to "help the dyslexic community engage with technology more effectively." His company specializes in healthcare and educational software. Earlier this year, we exchanged emails discussing the link between entrepreneurship and dyslexia.

Gary's advice is "whenever there is something you don't understand or struggle with, don't be afraid to ask for help or advice from people who have the solutions."

In the March 2015 issue of *Fast Company* the magazine mentioned a London-based designer who was dyslexic and obsessed with music. Because of his dyslexia, **Yurl Suzuki** could not read music, which gave him an idea. He created Ototo, which transforms any object into a musical instrument. Ototo debuted on Kickstarter in February of 2014 and was a success. It is sold at the Museum of Modern Art in New York City.

We are experiencing a Digital Renaissance in the dyslexic community as teens and young adults embrace entrepreneurship. These young startup founders and business owners are solving problems, creating products, and blazing new trails.

These startups represent a new era of dyslexic entrepreneurship as technology continues to open new doors there will be greater opportunities for the dyslexic individuals.

Do Not Sell Yourself Short and Never, Ever Settle!

"Dyslexics – the future is now; let's go change the world!"
My quote.

I would not trade being dyslexic for any amount of money. The majority of the dyslexics I interviewed for the book felt the same way. Our creative abilities and unique way of thinking is a gift. When I look through the list of dyslexic people past and present, I am truly honored to be part of this amazing group.

The importance is not how famous we are, or how many companies we own, what matters most is that each day we work to make a difference and create our own **"dent in the universe,"** as stated by Steve Jobs. I recently spoke to junior high students about entrepreneurship and pursuing their goals. At the end of my presentation I told the students, **"never sell yourself short or settle."**

There have been times in my life that I went against my better judgment and sold myself short. When I was growing up, the focus in school was on how to "fix" my weaknesses related to dyslexia: writing, reading, and spelling. There was little focus on my strengths. The goal was to find a way to mitigate the weaknesses and hide the dyslexia.

Often times, I felt like my brain was defective. I did not initially pursue a career that would have aligned my talents and dyslexic brain. As my career evolved I was able to start a small company and focus on finding a business model that allowed greater creative freedom.

From my experience of launching businesses and developing new products, I have learned that most businesses or entrepreneurial ventures fail for two reasons: lack of resiliency and lack of sales. When visiting with Pat Ryan, a retired dyslexic business owner and entrepreneur, he talked about how hard he worked and how he never gave up on himself, the business, or his employees.

Even during tough times, he worked his way through the "mud hole." Constantly talking to new customers and pitching your product takes resiliency not to give up when all you hear is "no."

Thomas Edison and other famous dyslexic inventors had hundreds of failed starts before they found success. Edison faced many defeated attempts before he found a formula that created the light bulb.

In the book *The Road Less Traveled* Dr. Peck says that how we value our time is related to how we value ourselves. He discussed how one of his patients did not value her time because she did not value herself. Once she gained an awareness of her behavior and the underlining cause, her behavior changed as she learned to value herself and her time.

Our dyslexic brains have value.

They are a unique gift even with their squiggly wiring and misfires. When our self-confidence takes a hit, especially when a customer or follower on social media says something tacky, we must remember that our brains are not defective. When we use our dyslexic brains to their full potential, the results can be amazing.

Beyond the competitive edge, I believe dyslexia can help provide us with a rich and engaging life. The most important thing I have learned is to focus less on the roadblocks and more on how to use the dyslexia to my advantage.

As outliers, we can provide a different perspective. In our rapidly changing world, our creative visual processing skills, along with the ability to conceptualize the whole picture, will increase in demand.

For business owners, entrepreneurs, and professionals, understanding how to leverage the value of dyslexia is essential.

Daniel Pink wrote about how dyslexics will have a huge advantage in our new economy. What matters most is determining which skills are timeless and which are quickly becoming obsolete. In Pink's book *The Whole New Mind* he mentioned a study conducted by the Federal Reserve Bank of Dallas. The employment data analyzed by the Fed demonstrated that jobs in the future will require emotional intelligence, imagination, and creativity. All of these characteristics are typical in a dyslexic individual. Tasks and processes that can be done by a robot or computer will be automated. Think about it, five years ago most of us would have laughed at the thought of self-driving cars or living on Mars. Today, there are companies working to make these ideas a reality.

Our time is now. To go and blaze new trails big and small, to create, to invent, and most of all, celebrate the brilliance within the dyslexic brain.

I close this book with one of my favorite ads from Apple, which I believe is the Ode to Dyslexics Everywhere – the infamous Apple advertising campaign.

"Here's to the crazy ones.

The misfits.
The rebels.
The troublemakers.
The round pegs in the square holes.
The ones who think differently.
They're not fond of rules.
And they have no respect for status quo.
You can praise them, disagree with them, quote them, disbelieve them, glorify them, vilify them.
About the only thing you can't do is ignore them.
Because they change things.
They invent. They imagine. They heal.
They explore. They create. They inspire.
They push the human race forward.
Maybe they have to be crazy.

How else can you stare at an empty canvas and see a work of art?

Or sit in silence and hear a song that's never been written.

Or gaze at a red planet and see a laboratory on wheels.

We make tools for these people.

While some see them as crazy ones, we see genius.

Because people who are crazy enough to think they can change the world are the ones who do."

To the Dyslexic Community – Let's go change the world!

Dyslexia Resources

Books
Overcoming Dyslexia by Sally Shaywitz, M.D.
The Gift of Dyslexia by Ronald D. Davis
In the Mind's Eye by Thomas West
The Dyslexic Advantage by Brock L. Eide, M.D., M.A and
Fernette F. Eide, M.D.

Blogs
In the Mind's Eye Dyslexia Renaissance Blog http://
inthemindseyedyslexicrenaissance.blogspot.com/

Movies
Dislexckia The Movie
http://www.dislecksiathemovie.com/

The Big Picture Movie – Rethinking Dyslexia
http://thebigpicturemovie.com/

Dyslexia – Entrepreneurship and Business Resources

Books
Like a Virgin: Secrets They Won't Teach You at Business School by Richard Branson
Mission in a Bottle by Seth Goldman & Barry Nalebuff
The Four Steps to the Epiphany by Steven Gary Blank
Do More Faster by David Cohen and Brad Feld
The Lean Startup by Eric Ries
Crossing The Chasm by Geoffrey A. Moore
The Icarus Deception by Seth Godin

YouTube Videos and Channels
Mark Cuban, Multiple interviews on YouTube

Daniel Pink, Whole New Mind
https://www.youtube.com/watch?v=RFL30u5BdLc

Richard Branson
https://www.youtube.com/channel/
UCza0aKF6sBN8OYQBHqz_YNQ

The Dyslexic Advantage
https://www.youtube.com/channel/
UCoWXpxHzlAdf7zHem1kGRRA

Tom West, Author of *In the Mind's Eye* and *Thinking Like Einstein*
https://www.youtube.com/watch?v=grZQhqTZUZQ

Dr. Julie Logan, Dyslexia and Entrepreneurship Presentation
https://www.youtube.com/watch?v=i0NQcljwdKI

Tiffany Sunday
https://www.youtube.com/user/TiffanySunday1

Crowdfunding
Kickstarter is an all or nothing platform. It is the most popular crowdfunding platform. However, it can be very difficult to raise large sums of money for a new business venture.

Key point to remember, if you do not raise the full amount requested during the fund raising campaign, the money is refunded. Kickstarter does not allow personal campaigns. www.kickstarter.com

GoFundMe is for personal campaigns. What I like best about this platform is that you can keep the money donated less a 10 percent processing fee. I used GoFundMe twice to pre-sell my books. The funds raised were used to pay the editors. www.gofundme.com

Articles or Blog Posts

How Being Dyslexic Can Help Shape Entrepreneurs by Seth Goldman
http://www.inc.com/seth-goldman/how-being-dyslexic-helps-shape-entrepreneurs.html

Portrait of the Not-So-Average Inc. 500 CEO, Inc. Magazine, September 2014
http://www.inc.com/magazine/201409/leigh-buchanan/inc.500-introduction-to-the-2014-winners.html

Trust Can Scale by Chris Moody
http://www.feld.com/archives/2013/02/trust-can-scale.html

Meetup Groups and Dyslexia Associations

Dyslexic Entrepreneurs and Professionals Meetup
http://www.meetup.com/Dyslexic-Entrepreneurs-and-Professionals/members/

British Dyslexia Association teamed with Good Story to provide mentoring to young dyslexic entrepreneurs ages 18-30. For more information, send an email to hi@good-story.org.uk

Startup Blogs

Richard Branson, Founder of Virgin http://www.virgin.com/richard-branson

Mark Suster, Former Entrepreneur http://www.bothside-softhetable.com/

Fred Wilson, Venture Capitalist http://avc.com/about

Alex Muse, Entrepreneur http://www.startupmuse.com/blog-2/

Eric Ries, Entrepreneur http://www.startuplessons-learned.com/

Brad Feld, Entrepreneur http://www.feld.com/

Blogging
WordPress www.wordpress.org

Podcasts
The Codpast was created by Sean Douglas. He hosts podcast talk show that focuses the creative aspect of the dyslexic brain. https://thecodpast.wordpress.com/

Dyslexic Management Companies
Half Penny Development is a human resources and personal development company that focuses on educating employers about dyslexia and helping dyslexic employees. http://www.halfpennydevelopment.co.uk/

Online Media
Mashable www.mashable.com
Tech Crunch www.techcrunch.com
Venture Beat www.venturebeat.com

Leadership and Executive Coaching Resources

Books

The Virgin Way Everything I Know About Leadership by Richard Branson

9 Things You Simply Must Do, Necessary Endings, and Integrity by Dr. Henry Cloud

Good to Great by Jim Collins

Accountability: The Key to Driving a High-Performance Culture by Greg Bustin

Blog Posts

Best Mentor Relationships Eventually Become Two Way
http://www.feld.com/archives/2014/09/mentors-618-best-mentor-relationships-eventually-become-two-way.html

Mentorship and Entrepreneurship
http://www.entrepreneur.com/article/228990

Mentors Are the Secret Weapons of Successful Startups
http://techcrunch.com/2015/03/22/mentors-are-the-secret-weapons-of-successful-startups/

Organizations
Vistage International is a business leadership, executive coaching, and mentoring organization. http://www.vistage.com/

Executive Coaches
Jeff Govoni is an executive coach and owner of Springtide Leadership Development http://springtideleadership.com/

Doug Moran is an executive coach and author of *If You Will Lead.* http://www.ifyouwilllead.com/

Startups
Score is a non-profit organization that connects retired experts with startup founders and new business owners. https://www.score.org/

Startup Mentor Programs
Virgin Startup Mentorship Program helps young entrepreneurs and new business owners in the United Kingdom. http://www.virginstartup.org/mentoring/become-a-mentor/

Think About the Future Resources

Books

A Whole New Mind and *Free Agent Nation* by Daniel Pink
Ctrl Alt Delete by Mitch Joel
The Shallows: What the Internet is Doing to Our Brains by Nicholas Carr
Lights in the Tunnel by Martin Ford
The Singularity is Near by Ray Kurzeil
You Posted What!? by Tiffany Sunday

Blogs

Steve Few, Visual Business Intelligence http://www.perceptualedge.com/

Online Media

Wired Magazine www.wired.com
CNET News http://www.cnet.com/news/
The Verge http://www.theverge.com/tech

Inspirational and Personal Development Resources

Books
The 7 Habits of Highly Effective People by Stephen Covey
Napoleon Hill's Keys to Success Edited by Matthew Sartwell
Man's Search for Meaning by Viktor E. Frankl
Running and Being by Dr. George Sheeham

Blog Posts and Articles
My Secret to Life Is to Dream Big & Think Positive by Troy Marshall
http://beefmagazine.com/blog/my-secret-life-dream-big-think-positive

Stop Stealing Dreams by Seth Godin
http://www.sethgodin.com/sg/docs/stopstealingdreams-screen.pdf

Thought Leaders
Chris Brogan www.chrisbrogan.com

David Meerman Scott www.davidmeermanscott.com

Seth Godin www.sethgodin.com

Penelope Truck www.penelopetrunk.com

Verbal Communication and Speaking
Toastmasters International https://www.toastmasters.org/

YouTube
Steve Jobs - Stanford Commencement Speech 2005
https://www.youtube.com/watch?v=D1R-jKKp3NA

TED Talks
TED is a platform for spreading new ideas. Everyone who speaks at TED is selected by a panel with the goal of spreading new ideas or providing an alternative approach to an old idea or practice. www.ted.com

Brene Brown – The Power of Vulnerability
https://www.youtube.com/watch?v=iCvmsMzlF7o

St. Ken Robinson – How Schools Kill Creativity
https://www.youtube.com/watch?v=iG9CE55wbtY

Mel Robbins – How to Stop Screwing Yourself Over by Mel Robbins https://www.youtube.com/watch?v=Lp7E973zozc

Digital Technology Tools for Dyslexics

The best way to find digital tools is to search the Internet for dyslexia non-profit organizations or similar groups. These organizations frequent post information about new digital tools developed for dyslexics.

Learning Ally is a non-profit that assists individuals who are reading impaired.   The organization offers a wide selection of audio books for students and adults. https://www.learningally.org/

BrainbookLive is a Social Network for dyslexics created by Gary Smith. http://www.brainbook.co.uk/

Dyslexia Toolbox is a cross-platform app designed to help dyslexics manage their daily life more efficiently. Features included in the app are colored overlay system and the ability to transfer text to a more readable format.   https://itunes.apple.com/gb/app/dyslexia-toolbox/id847765304?mt=8&ign-mpt=uo%3D2

Read and Focus Cards is an app applies the same principal of using a note card or bookmarker to help dyslexics focus on the text they are reading. http://www.focusandread.com/

Read and Focus iTunes App
https://itunes.apple.com/us/app/read-and-focus/id920617853?mt=12

IntoWords is an iTunes app that can be used on an iPad. The app converts emails, texts, and

United States iPad App
https://itunes.apple.com/us/app/intowords/id639521056?mt=8

UK iPad App
https://itunes.apple.com/gb/app/intowords/id593475776?mt=8

Here is a link to an Into Words app product demonstration video on YouTube. https://www.youtube.com/watch?v=Nb6xRf2Wj4E

Bibliography

Beck, Melinda, 2013. "Dyslexia Workarounds: Creativity Without a Lot of Reading," *The Wall Street Journal* April 2.

http://www.wsj.com/articles/SB1000142412788732402 05045783964213828251 96

Bort, Julie, 2014. "Cisco CEO John Chambers: My Dyslexia Is a Weakness AND a Strength," *Business Insider* October 8.

http://www.businessinsider.com/cisco-ceo-john-chambers-talks-dyslexia-2014-7

Bowers, Brett, 2014. "Study Shows Stronger Link Between Entrepreneurs and Dyslexia," *The New York Times* October 29.

http://www.nytimes.com/2007/12/05/business/worldbusiness/05iht-dyslexia.4.8602036.html

Buchanan, Leigh, 2014. "Inside the Mind of the Entrepreneur," *Inc.* Magazine September.

http://www.inc.com/magazine/201409/leigh-buchanan/inc.500-introduction-to-the-2014-winners.html

De Santillana, Giorgio "Leonard da Vinci" Reynal & Company Inc. 1956

Gellman, Lindsay and Brown, Eliot, 2015. "WeWork: Now a $5 Billion Co-Working Startup," *The Wall Street Journal* January 28.

http://www.wsj.com/articles/wework-now-a-5-billion-real-estate-sartup-1418690163

Goldman, Seth, 2014. "How Being Dyslexic Can Help Shape Entrepreneurs," *Inc.* Magazine October 22.

http://www.inc.com/welcome.html?destination=http://www.inc.com/seth-goldman/how-being-dyslexic-helps-shape-entrepreneurs.html

Konrad, Alex, 2014. "Capitalist Communes," *Forbes* November 24.

http://www.forbes.com/sites/alexkonrad/2014/11/05/the-rise-of-wework/

Lawson, Sarah, 2015. "Maker Music Ototo Lets You Have Your Cake and Eat It Too," *Fast Company* March.

http://www.fastcodesign.com/3041524/wanted/ maker-music

Loffe, Yevgeny, 2014. "Q&A With Brett Kopf Co-Founder and CEO of Remind," *EdTech Times* May 22

http://edtechtimes.com/2014/05/22/qa-brett-kopf-co-founder-ceo-remind101/

Logan, Julie PhD., 2010. "Unusual Talent: a Study of Successful Leadership and Delegation in Dyslexic Entrepreneurs," Case Business School, London August.

http://www.cassknowledge.com/research/article/ unusual-talent-study-successful-leadership-and-delegation-dyslexic-entrepreneurs

Werdigier, Julia, 2013. "Relying on Gut Instinct to Run a Business," *The New York Times* June 9.

http://www.nytimes.com/2013/06/10/business/ global/10iht-manager10.html?_r=0

West, Thomas G., 2014. "'Amazing Shortcomings, Amazing Strengths' Beginning to Understand the Hidden Talents of Dyslexics," *Asian Pacific Journal of Developmental Differences* Vol. 1 No.1 January.

GoFundMe Acknowledgments

Gold
Skip Howard
Eric McGehearty
Bill Murray

Silver
Warren Burns
Lauren Ward

Supporter
Heather Hardeman

Author's Acknowledgments

My lifelong dream was to be a journalist, author, film director, and entrepreneur. Selecting a lifetime career seemed too limiting when I was a teenager, and I still feel the same way now. We live in one of the most exciting periods in history and have access to more opportunities than ever before. In many ways, this book is a celebration of dyslexia and how we can use our dyslexic brain to create, innovate, and solve complex problems.

Thank you written on these pages does not seem big enough to express my gratitude to everyone who helped make this book possible. I gained so much from this experience. Writing this book validated my personal mission of inspiring fellow dyslexics.

To my father, Gerry Sunday – thank you for your support and taking the time to edit the book. Once again, this book is in memory of my late mother, Judy Sunday, who shared with me the gift of learning and taught me to believe in myself.

To my son, Brandon Belanger – your support and feedback was invaluable. This book is for you – to understand early that we are *just different* and know nothing is really broken. You are part of the next generation of dyslexic entrepreneurs.

To Mary Lewis – thank you for reviewing the book and offering your insight and edits. I truly appreciate your feedback!

To Sabrina Hancock – thank you for all your hard work editing and double checking resources, commas, and links. Your work made this book stronger!

This book would not have been possible without the help and support of the dyslexic community and the following people: Skip Howard, Seth Goldman, Pat Ryan, Aimee Gordon, Heather Hardeman, Eric McGehearty, Heather McGehearty, Gary Smith, Greg Bustin, Barry Goldberg, Lauren Ward, Doug Moran, Jeff Govoni, Ryan Kinzy, Ellen O'Neill, Steve Few, Thomas G. West, Dr. Julie Logan, Warren Burns, Andres Traslavina, and Bill Murray.

To my editing team, Julie Richie, Sabrina Hancock, and Megan Hancock – thank you for your insight and editing oversight!

Once again, this book represents a village of support from friends, family, and the dyslexic community. I greatly appreciate everyone's time and help.

About the Author

Tiffany Sunday is a dyslexic entrepreneur, business owner, speaker, and author of *You Posted What!?* She has been starting businesses and developing new products since junior high.

Tiffany speaks frequently at business and educational events, advising organizations and companies on the topics of entrepreneurship, dyslexia, and our digital transformation.

Tiffany plans to write and publish two more books in 2015.

- *Dyslexic Teens – How to Start A Business or Launch a Career Before High School Graduation*
- *Why Wait?! How to Start a Business Before College*

She crowd-funded and self-published her first book, *You Posted What!?,* which discussed how teens and young adults use the Internet and social media to start businesses or launch their careers before college graduation.

She has appeared on ABC, NBC, CNN Radio, and in *The Dallas Morning News, The Dallas Business Journal,* and *Restaurant News*. Tiffany lives in Dallas, Texas with her son Brandon.

For more information about Tiffany, please visit http://www.tiffanysunday.com.

Made in the USA
San Bernardino, CA
19 September 2015